BUTTERFLIES
OF THE
WORLD

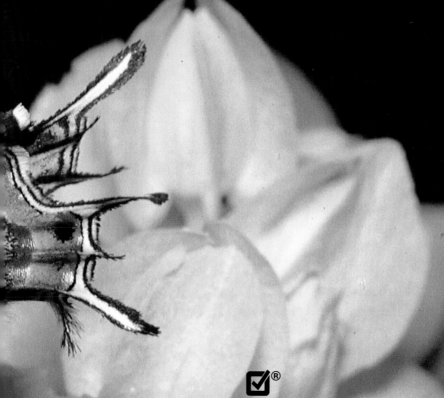

BUTTERFLIES
OF THE
WORLD

Rod and Ken Preston-Mafham

☑®
Facts On File, Inc.

Butterflies of the World

Copyright © 1988 & 1999 Cassell plc
Text copyright © 1988 & 1999 Rod & Ken Preston-Mafham
Photographs copyright 1988 & 1999 © Premaphotos Wildlife Ltd

This Facts On File edition published in 2004 by Cassell Illustrated,
a member of the Octopus Publishing Group, 2-4 Heron Quays,
London E14 4JP

Facts On File, Inc.
132 West 31st Street
New York NY 10001

For Library of Congress Cataloging-in-Publication data, please
contact Facts On File.

ISBN: 0-8160-5713-3

Facts On File books are available at special discounts when
purchased in bulk quantities for businesses, associations, institutions,
or sales promotions. Please call our Special Sales Department in
New York at (212) 967-8800 or (800) 322-8755.

You can find Facts On File on the World Wide Web at
http://www.factsonfile.com

Printed in China

_____ _____ 10 9 8 7 6 5 4 3 2 1

This book is printed on acid-free paper.

Contents

Preface

When we were asked to write the present volume, our second in the 'of the World' series, our first concern was how to write an original book on butterflies. Our thoughts inevitably turned to bookshop shelves already creaking under the weight of butterfly books, including virtual encyclopedias of voluminous information. At first sight it appeared that we would find it difficult to present anything original in any work which we could possibly contemplate writing. However, after due consideration we saw that the wisest approach was to present a certain amount of subject matter based on well-known and sound research, encompassing the kind of background material necessary in any serious book on the biology of butterflies, seasoned with a rich sprinkling of unique anecdotal material gleaned mainly by Ken on his wide-ranging travels around the world. In a work of this size, intended to give an overall insight into the subject, it is sadly inevitable that an enormous amount of relevant information has to be omitted, simply on the grounds of space, and we have therefore been forced to be very selective in choosing the material for presentation. This has meant leaving out, or considering only briefly, some well-researched scientific observations. Instead, we have included many personal observations which, although not as scientifically valid as properly conducted research, nevertheless might add something to our growing body of knowledge on butterfly behaviour, as well as communicating in some small measure the excitement of observing butterflies in the tropics. Many readers will be limited to first-hand experience of the butterflies of Europe or North America, so we felt justified in biasing the text towards tropical butterflies, especially when dealing with personal anecdotal observations.

Mindful of the fact that many butterfly enthusiasts are also interested in other forms of insect life and may already own a number of books thereon, we have chosen the illustrations with some care in order to ensure that none has previously appeared in print. In our picture library at *Premaphotos Wildlife* we currently hold 2,300 colour slides of butterflies covering 405 species, mostly depicted in the adult stage. Every one of these photographs, including the pictures in the present work, was taken by the authors without resorting to the use of captured or bred specimens or any kind of human interference designed to obtain a picture, thus following our broad philosophy that wildlife photography should portray animals living wild and free in their natural environment. The fact that we have managed to amass such a large number of photographs from around the world, often under difficult conditions, should be a considerable stimulus to any readers who have considered photographing butterflies in the field but have been disillusioned by hearing or reading about the difficulties intrinsic in such an exercise. You should also bear in mind that our coverage of butterflies has been compiled as part of a much greater coverage of the world's plant and animal life, a time-consuming occupation which has often left only a small percentage of our effort to be dedicated to butterfly photography. Anyone willing to go out into the field and restrict their attentions solely to butterflies would therefore have an excellent chance of achieving a great degree of success.

In writing this book, we have employed two different approaches in that the early chapters, which contain basic, background information on butterflies as a group, have been written in the third person; whereas much of the rest of the book has been written in the first person, mainly by Ken. We would also like to take the opportunity to justify what might appear to be the over-frequent use in the text of 'possibly', 'probably', 'often' and other words implying a measure of uncertainty. The more that we learn about butterflies the more we realise just how little we understand of their daily lives, despite the long popularity of collecting them. There is much disagreement among different groups of researchers concerning the reasons for certain types of behaviour or physiological adaptations, and even more over the interpretation of experimental data. This work is not aimed at the expert lepidopterist and we therefore make no apology for the occasional anthropomorphism where it is used to enlighten the uninitiated reader who may find scientific jargon difficult to comprehend.

In travelling around the world in pursuit of our wildlife subjects we have been fortunate to enjoy the assistance of numerous, generous people to whom we offer our grateful thanks. In particular we must mention Dr Gerardo Lamas, Peru; Dr Vitor Becker, Brazil; Adriana Hoffmann, Chile; Prof. Gilberto Rios, Cecilia de Blohm, Venezuela; Dr Mario Boza, Costa Rica; Dr Angus McCrae, Kenya and England; Ken Proud, Java; Ken Scriven, WWF Malaysia; Dr Roger Kitching, Australia; Dr John Ismay, New Guinea; Dr Amnon Freidberg, Israel; Dr Thomas Emmell, USA, to whom we offer special thanks. We also thank Rod's wife Jean, our computer expert, who taught us the ins and outs of the word-processor on which the manuscript was prepared.

Rod and Ken Preston-Mafham

Chapter 1

Introduction to the Butterflies

Butterflies are members of the insect order Lepidoptera, the literal meaning of which is 'scale-winged', and included with them are the moths. It is the wing scales which give the butterflies their beautiful colours and patterns and make them one of the most familiar of all insect groups. The exact origins and age of the Lepidoptera are not precisely known, since the fossilisation of such delicate creatures has occurred only rarely, but fossils of some primitive moths in amber have been dated as originating in the Lower Cretaceous period between 100 and 130 million years ago. This fits in quite well with the estimated age of the flowering plants alongside which it is assumed that the Lepidoptera have evolved, since all but a few of them depend upon flowers as a source of food as adults. The closest relatives of the butterflies and moths are believed to be the caddis flies of the order Trichoptera, both these and the Lepidoptera having probably evolved from a common ancestor. The exact number of members of the Lepidoptera in existence is not precisely known, since new species are still being discovered and described. The likely number is in the region of 160,000 of which about 20,000 are butterflies and the remainder moths. This makes them one of the most diverse groups of living organisms and within the insects only the beetles exceed them in the number of species to be found today.

Like the beetles, the butterflies and moths belong to a sub-division of the insects called the Endopterygota, in which there are four distinct phases in the life-cycle, namely egg, larva, pupa and adult. The more primitive sub-division, the Exopterygota, includes insects such as the locusts, in which the egg is followed by a series of instars, each of which is a wingless miniature of the adult, the final instar moulting into the adult proper. The apparent advantage of the endopterygote type of life-cycle is that the young utilise a totally different food source from that of the adults and as a result there is no competition between them. The disadvantage is that the soft-bodied butterfly caterpillar is very vulnerable to both parasitisation and predation with the result that some very interesting adaptations, discussed in later chapters, have evolved to cope with these problems.

The separation of the Lepidoptera into the butterflies and the moths is a somewhat artificial one, since although most butterflies are recognisable clearly as such and most moths similarly so, there are some of each which do not fit so neatly into this tidy pattern. As an example, one usually thinks of butterflies as being day-flying with clubbed antennae and moths as nocturnal with feathery antennae, but where do the day-flying moths with clubbed antennae fit into this simple classification? Despite these problems it is possible to construct a reasonably acceptable system of classification for the Lepidoptera, separating the butterflies and moths, and it is the characteristics of the major butterfly families which will be considered shortly. Before doing so, however, it might be useful if the workings of the biological classification system are looked at first.

Although many of the butterfly groups have common names, e.g. the Papilionidae are the swallowtails and the Lycaenidae are usually referred to as the blues (despite the fact that large numbers of them are not blue), relatively few of the twenty or so thousand butterflies in the world have a common name. Those which do are either easily recognisable, like the swallowtail in the UK, or there are so few species in a particular area that each is instantly recognisable, this being basically true for the British Isles. As a consequence, although some species might be referred to in the text by their common names, others can have only their species name.

The structured form of classification used worldwide is that developed by the Swede Linnaeus during the eighteenth century. In this system, the living world is divided up into a number of sections, each containing organisms with a fairly close relationship to each other, the final division being that of the species. A species is defined as a population of individuals which are very similar to each other and can breed successfully amongst themselves to produce fertile offspring. Taking the example of one of the world's largest butterflies, the giant birdwing butterfly, it is classified as a member of the animal kingdom in the following manner:

KINGDOM	Animalia
PHYLUM	Arthropoda
CLASS	Insecta
ORDER	Lepidoptera
FAMILY	Papilionidae
SUB-FAMILY	Papilioninae
GENUS	*Ornithoptera*
SPECIFIC NAME	*goliath*

Thus the species name of the birdwing butterfly is *Ornithoptera goliath*, all such names being italicised in the text. Whereas some genera have only one species, others contain many species which share the generic name but have their own specific names, e.g. *Ornithoptera alexandrae*, the world's largest butterfly, shares its generic name with *O. goliath*. The European swallowtail, on the other hand, is not a birdwing and is sufficiently different from them to be included in a separate genus, *Papilio*, to which many of the world's other swallowtails also belong. Bearing these rules in mind, the names given to the various butterflies discussed in the text should now be more easily understood.

Classification of the butterflies

Despite the fact that the butterflies are one of the most studied insect groups, there is no real concensus of opinion as to precisely how they should be classified and the system used here is based on that published in 1984 in the proceedings of the Symposium of the Royal Entomological Society of London, No. 11. In this system, the butterflies are sub-divided into two superfamilies, the Hesperioidea and the Papilionoidea, the former containing one family, the Hesperiidae, and the latter four families, the Papilionidae, the Pieridae, the Lycaenidae and the Nymphalidae. Each one of these families contains a number of sub-families, though not all of these will be discussed here.

Family Hesperiidae

These are usually referred to by the familiar name of 'skippers' on account of their rapid, erratic flight which resembles that of a moth more

Papilio phorcas. The green-patch swallowtail is a typical swallowtail butterfly with its 'tailed' hind wings. This specimen spent a few minutes basking in a sunlit patch in Kakamega Forest in western Kenya after a cool night of heavy rain.

than that of a butterfly. The similarity to the moths does not stop here for they tend to have the short, stout body of a moth with a broad head and wide-spaced antennae. Although they usually sit with their wings held closed above their backs in typical butterfly fashion, they also have the ability to hold their wings out to the side in the manner of a moth. They are separated into six sub-families with an estimated 3,500 species worldwide. Many of them, such as the typical European species, are coloured rather drab shades of brown, but some tropical species are very beautifully marked. Hesperiid larvae feed on a wide range of plant families and across the sub-families there is a tendency for them to form shelters, tubes or tunnels using the leaves of their food plants, within which they can lie concealed. Pupation takes place in a cocoon in which pieces of dried-up leaves are incorporated.

The sub-family Megathyminae are somewhat different from the more typical skippers and some taxonomists include them in a family of their own. They are called yucca skippers, since they feed upon yuccas and agaves of the plant family Agavaceae. Unlike the other hesperiids, they have the head narrower than the thorax and the antennae close together. The larvae are interesting in that they are root- and stem-borers of their host plants, a moth-like rather than butterfly-like habit. They eventually pupate in holes mined in the leaves, after first spinning a silken cocoon.

Family Papilionidae

Members of this family are collectively referred to as the swallowtails since the hind-wings of many members of the family have backward extensions resembling the streamers of a swallow's tail. Many members of the family are beautifully marked and coloured and included amongst them are the world's largest butterflies, the bird-wings, most of which come from New Guinea and the surrounding islands. Curiously, the majority of the bird-wings lack the characteristic swallow tail. The larvae of the swallowtails are unique in the possession of a structure, the osmeterium, details of which are discussed in a later chapter. The pupae are usually attached to a plant or other object by means of the cremaster, in a head-up manner supported by a silken girdle. There are three sub-families within the Papilionidae, one of which, the Baroniinae, contains but a single unusual species from Mexico.

Sub-family Parnassiinae

This small group of about 50 species is generally referred to as the apollos. They are not typical of the rest of the family in that they generally lack a swallowtail, the wings being rounded and semi-transparent, and the body is thickly covered in hair. The majority of apollos live at high levels in Europe and Asia and their slow lazy flight also distinguishes them from the typical, fast-flying swallowtails. The saxifrages, typical mountain plants, are included amongst those upon which the larvae feed.

Sub-family Papilioninae

This group of about 650 species is worldwide in distribution, though with its greatest numbers in the tropical regions of the Old World, and it contains the typical swallowtail butterflies. As a result of the relatively large numbers of species in this group, some lepidopterists recognise three sub-divisions within it, based upon shape and food plant. The true swallowtails are the typical members of the family with a very wide distribution; the kite swallowtails are so named on account of their wing shape, and the poison eaters get their name from the fact that their caterpillars feed upon the poisonous vines of the plant family Aristolochiaceae.

Family Pieridae

This family includes the well-known whites, the orange tips, the brimstones and the sulphurs, the majority of which are white or yellow in colour, though reds, browns and blues do appear in some members. The family as a whole totals about 1,000 species and their larvae are very uniform in shape and are naked or slightly hairy, lacking the external projections of other families. Most are coloured to match their backgrounds, though some, such as those of the large white, *Pieris brassicae*, are warningly coloured. The pupae adopt a similar coloration and lie head-up attached by the cremaster and the silken girdle. Of the four sub-families, three have sufficient members to be worth a separate mention.

Sub-family Dismorphiinae

This is a small group of mainly tropical butterflies, there being one European representative, in the wood white, *Leptidea sinapsis*. These butterflies have long narrow wings and slim bodies atypical of the rounded, robust appearance of the other pierids. The food plants are members of the Fabaceae, the pea and bean family, and I have observed the wood white ovipositing upon a birdsfoot trefoil plant in Warwickshire, England.

Sub-family Pierinae

The Pierinae have a worldwide distribution and contain about two-thirds of the total number of pierid butterflies. They are commonly called the whites and include such species as *Pieris brassicae* and *P. rapae*, both of which are pests of brassica crops in Europe. The African butterflies of the genus *Belenois* are migratory and often collect in extremely large numbers to drink on damp ground. The numbers involved in such a migration may be appreciated by studying the photograph of the South African migratory species *Belenois aurota*. The Pierinae also includes some brightly coloured species such as *Delias nigrina* from Australia but, in-

Delias nigrina.   The jezabels belonging to the same family as the large and small white butterflies are noted for the striking patterns on the undersides of their wings. This is probably a form of warning coloration and advertises distasteful properties. Photographed in subtropical rain forest in Lake Barrine National Park, Queensland, Australia.

terestingly, members of this particular genus are usually less colourful on the upper surfaces of the wings than on the lower. The food plants of the majority of the larvae within this sub-family are members of the Brassicaceae.

Sub-family Coliadinae

Whereas members of the previous sub-family are wholly or partly white, butterflies in this group are predominantly yellow in colour and include the brimstones and the sulphurs. About 250 species are known, the majority of which are tropical, the rest being cosmopolitan in distribution. Like the previous group, some species migrate in very large numbers and the clouded yellow butterfly, *Colias croceus*, often migrates in a

Thersamonia thersamon.   Lycaenids belonging to the sub-family Lycaeninae are commonly called coppers on account of the normal ground-colour of the upper wing surfaces. This is the lesser fiery copper, photographed in springtime on Israel's Mediterranean coast. The flower belongs to the cosmopolitan daisy family, Asteraceae, popular nectaring plants for butterflies because of the abundant nectar offered in the multiple florets which make up the composite flower-head.

good year from continental Europe to the British Isles. The larvae feed upon plants of the families Asteraceae and Fabaceae.

Family Lycaenidae

The Lycaenids are a large family of some 6,000 or more species, about 40 per cent of all butterflies, with a worldwide distribution, though they exist in their greatest numbers in tropical regions. On the whole they are small, brightly coloured butterflies and include the blues, the hairstreaks and the coppers. Many tropical species possess tails, often in the form of a false head, the role of which will be discussed in a later chapter. The larvae are sometimes described as being slug-like, though in fact they bear a greater resemblance to a legless woodlouse, so that in some texts they are referred to as onisciform. They may be slightly hairy and are most often green or brown in colour and many species live in interesting associations with ants. One researcher, on making a survey of the Lycaenidae, found in fact that about one-third of those butterflies whose life histories had been studied had a larva which associated in some way with ants. The importance of this ant/larva relationship to the lycaenids will be discussed later. Like the larvae the pupae tend to be short and broad and they lack a cremaster so that they either lie free on the ground or remain attached to the host plant by means of a silken girdle. Ten sub-families are recognised according to the system being followed, though only the major ones will be discussed.

Sub-family Theclinae

The Theclinae are often referred to as the hairstreaks on account of the delicate lines on the underside of the wings. They have a worldwide distribution but occur in their greatest variety in South America where some extremely beautiful species are to be found. A number of species have so-called 'false heads' in that the rear wing is marked with an eye-spot at its hindmost extremity and from the wings grow one or more extensions which resemble the antennae and front legs of the butterfly. The larvae feed upon a variety of plant families, including some trees, and a few feed upon plant bugs and ant regurgitations, at least in the later instars.

Sub-family Lycaeninae

Commonly called the coppers, because of the inclusion of a lovely copper colour on the top sides of the wings, they have relatively fewer species than some of the other groups within the Lycaenidae. They are distributed mainly across the temperate regions of the northern hemisphere, though a few exist in other parts of the world. Larvae of this sub-family should be sought on members of the plant family Polygonaceae, the docks and sorrels.

Sub-family Polyommatinae

This sub-family is often called the blues since this is the predominant colour in many of its members. These butterflies have representatives in most parts of the world but they exist in their greatest variety in the temperate regions of the northern hemisphere where they are often found in great abundance in areas of grassland. The larvae feed on quite a variety of plant families and whereas some species are restricted to only one type of plant, others, such as the holly blue, have been found on a wide variety of different plant hosts. Some larvae, such as those of the European large blue butterfly, feed on plant food in their early stages but on ant larvae later on.

Sub-family Riodininae

This sub-family, called the metalmarks on account of the seemingly metallic raised areas on the wings of some species, may also be referred to as a separate family, the Riodinidae, or even the Nemeobiidae in some literature. This problem arises from the difficulties that butterfly tax-onomists have had in placing this group in relation to the other butterfly families. Members of the group show a great deal of variation in shape, some species resembling moths, while others have long tails on the hind wings giving them a superficial resemblance to the swallowtails. They also show a lot of variation in coloration, having some of the most beautiful patterns and most brilliant colours of any of the butterflies. Unfortunately these are not often seen by man, since many species have the habit of sitting under leaves out of sight or else they fly high up, out of sight in the forest canopy. The majority of the 1,000 or so species are indeed forest dwellers from South and Central America, though some are found in other parts of the world, including North America, and even Europe boasts one species, the Duke of Burgundy, *Hamearis lucina*. The larvae are onisciform, green, whitish or sometimes red in colour, often clothed with fine hairs and some have brightly coloured protuberances. Like the adults, the pupae are very variable in that some hang freely by the tail while others are more typical of the lycaenids and are attached to leaves by a silk girdle.

Family Nymphalidae

The Nymphalidae is a very large family with about 6,000 species be-longing to 13 sub-families which between them have a cosmopolitan distribution. Each sub-family tends to be relatively distinctive in its characteristics and in some classification systems they are given full family status. They are, however, tied together by one very distinctive characteristic which is that the front pair of legs are so reduced that they cannot be used for walking and in males especially they are reduced to a hairy pad. This reduction is clearly very noticeable as, during a re-cent discussion on butterflies that I had with some eleven-year-olds, one

Caria mantinea. Members of the sub-family Riodininae are called metalmarks, a name derived from the seemingly metallic raised areas which are conspicuous features of the wings of many species. The butterfly pictured here illustrates the point particularly well and is a common species in the fabulously rich rain forest at Tingo Maria in Peru.

Apodemia mormo. Only a few species of metalmarks or riodinines manage to penetrate northwards to the United States from their centre of distribution in tropical South and Central America. The Mormon metalmark is a local species found in the deserts of south-west USA. This specimen was photographed in semi-desert near Tombstone, Arizona.

Caligo eurilochus.   The owl-butterflies of the sub-family Brassolinae number some 80 species, restricted to Central and South America. They are among the largest of all butterflies, and can easily be mistaken for bats when following their usual habit of flying near dusk. The caterpillars are sometimes pests in banana plantations, and this particular adult is perched on a banana leaf with the stem of another banana forming the out-of-focus background. Photographed in a clearing in tropical rain forest in Henry Pittier National Park, Venezuela.

of them asked how it was that a hibernating small tortoiseshell butterfly in her garage had lost its front legs, which of course it had not. The other important characteristic of all of the Nymphalidae is that the pupa hangs head-first by its cremaster from a silk pad or, in some instances, lies on the ground. Of the thirteen sub-families, two are represented by only a single genus with restricted distributions, one being from China, the other from New Guinea. The other sub-families will now be considered in greater detail.

Sub-family Brassolinae

These are the so-called owl butterflies and their roughly 80 species are found exclusively in Central and South America. In general they are quite large butterflies with some members of the genus *Caligo* approaching the papilionid birdwings in size. The upper surfaces of the wings are often shades of brown in colour although in a few species this may be suffused with deep blue or purple, sometimes with yellow lines. The underside is usually cryptically marked and there is often a large, staring eye-marking in the centre of each hind wing. They are mainly denizens of the tropical forests, flying slowly and lazily around at dawn and dusk and remaining hidden during daytime. The larvae are smooth and usually have a forked tail segment. Those of the genus *Caligo* are gregarious and their main food is banana leaves, to the extent that they may become a serious pest in banana plantations. Larvae of other genera feed upon a variety of plant families, including grasses.

Sub-family Amathusiinae

This group have a number of common names, saturns and palmkings being but two. They are almost exclusively Indo-Australian in distribution, numbering about 100 species. Many of them bear a superficial resemblance to the morphos and owl butterflies of South America. Some have similar habits to those of the latter group in that they fly mainly at dawn and dusk and are pests in banana plantations. The larvae are noticeably hairy and possess a forked tail segment and, in most species, two elongated processes on the head. Their food preferences are in general very similar to those of the owl butterflies.

Sub-family Morphinae

This is another sub-family which is found only in South and Central America and it has about 70 species within it. The morphos, as they are called, are in the main very distinctive butterflies and they include some of the largest species found in their region of the world. Virtually all of them have rows of eyespots on the underside but it is the upper surface of a number of them which attracts most attention from lepidopterists. The reason is that the whole surface is coloured in a beautiful metallic blue, which seems to lift off almost like blue flames as the butterfly flaps lazily around a forest clearing. Other species are less noticeable, with the upper sides of the wings brown, brown and yellow, or the very palest green. The larvae are smooth, with tufts of hair along their backs and they feed upon grasses and members of the pea family.

Sub-family Satyrinae

This is a very large sub-family with a worldwide distribution and it contains about 1,500 species. They are commonly referred to as the browns, since this is the predominant colour of the group as a whole, and many species have distinctive eyespots on the upper wing surfaces. A small proportion of them have much brighter colours and marked patterns and they include some very beautiful species. The larvae are smooth, with a forked tail segment and they feed mainly upon grasses and sedges.

Sub-family Charaxinae

A cursory glance at the short, broad bodies and compact wings of many charaxids indicates a powerful flying machine and this is indeed the case with these butterflies. Couple this with some beautiful patterns and marvellous colours and one has an outstanding sub-family. In contrast to the striking upper wing patterns, some species, such as *Anaea archidona* from Columbia, are superb dead-leaf mimics with their wings closed. The group are mainly tropical in distribution, with between 300–400 species, just a few representatives being found in temperate regions. The larvae are smooth, usually with a pair of processes on the head and a bifid tail segment and the main plant families upon which they feed include the Fabaceae, Convolvulaceae and Euphorbiaceae.

Sub-family Heliconiinae

Almost all of the members of this sub-family have characteristic long, narrow wings, warningly coloured on both upper and lower surfaces, a long, slim body and very long antennae. With the exception of a few species in the southern USA, all of them come from the tropical regions of South and Central America, though it has recently been suggested that two genera from tropical Asia, whose caterpillars utilise the same food plants, should also be included in the Heliconiinae. A total of just under 70 species have been described to date. The larvae have rows of spines on which there are stiff bristles and their sole food plants are vines of the family Passifloraceae. The apparent co-evolution of these butterflies and their host plants has produced some interesting behavioural patterns which will be discussed in a later chapter.

Sub-family Ithomiinae

Many of the ithomiines bear a superficial resemblance to the preceding

Charaxes pleione. Members of the sub-family Charaxinae are much prized by collectors for their splendid markings, especially on the undersides of the wings. The topsides are rarely exposed to view for long, as the butterflies normally feed and roost with their wings closed. This male paused briefly to bask in a sunspot after spending some time feeding at dung on the cool floor of Kenya's Kakamega Forest.

Pierella hyalinus. Butterflies belonging to the sub-family Satyrinae are usually called browns, a title referring to the drab coloration characteristic of the group as whole. However, in the tropics, and especially in South America, many species have developed much more striking colours, the butterfly figured being a typical example. It prefers the gloomier parts of the forest, and was photographed basking, a rare occupation, on a leaf in a disused cocoa plantation at the SIMLA biological station in Trinidad's Northern Range.

Heliconius charithonia.   Butterflies of the sub-family Heliconiinae typically have long narrow wings which bear warning patterns on both surfaces. Only two species penetrate northwards into the USA from the group's stronghold in the Neotropical realm, this being one. Just over 70 species have been described to date, the larvae restricting their attentions to passion flowers.

Acraea natalica.   Although, like ithomiines and heliconiines, members of the group have long narrow wings, slender bodies and warning colours, this species shows a clinal variation over its vast range in Africa, the West African forms showing a high degree of melanism compared with the southern form illustrated, from South Africa's Drakensberg Mountains in the Transvaal.

Idea hypermnestra.   The huge slow-flying danaines of this genus are noted for the striking black and white network which patterns their wings, an example of warning coloration which advertises their distasteful properties. Photographed in Pasoh Forest Reserve in Malaysia.

sub-family, for they too have long, narrow wings and an even longer, slim abdomen and long antennae. Again, like the heliconiines, they are mainly warningly coloured on both wing surfaces and, indeed, since both sub-families occupy similar habitats in South and Central America they may easily be confused with each other in the field. An unusual characteristic of the present sub-family is that some species, such as *Ithomia pellucida*, have large transparent areas on the wings. The local name for this particular species is, in fact, the blue transparent. More than 300 species of Ithomiinae have so far been recognised. The larvae are smooth and have coloured patterns, their food plants being members of the poisonous Apocyanaceae and Solanaceae.

Sub-family Acraeinae

In some ways this sub-family is the African equivalent of the Heliconiinae and Ithomiinae in that, again, its members have long, slender wings and abdomens and fairly long antennae. Although about 200 of the 250 or so species are indeed African, there are representatives of the sub-family in both South America and the Indo-Australian region. The majority of species exhibit warning coloration and the larvae, like the heliconiine larvae they resemble, are spiny and feed upon poisonous members of the Passifloraceae in Africa. Those species which live outside Africa, however, feed upon a range of other plant families.

Sub-family Danainae

The Danainae include the well-known milkweed or monarch butterflies and they are mainly tropical or sub-tropical in distribution, numbering around 300 species. Some of them are migratory and probably the best known of these is the very widely distributed *Danaus plexippus* which extends into temperate regions and even ends up on occasions in the British Isles. Although the majority of species are warningly coloured in contrasting browns, oranges, yellows and whites, the genus *Idea* from the Old World is beautifully marked in black and white. The larvae are smooth, conspicuously marked in warning colours and may have one or more pairs of fleshy tubercles along their backs. They feed upon poisonous members of the plant families Asclepiadaceae, Apocyanaceae and Moraceae.

Sub-family Libytheinae

Although only a small group with just ten species, they have a world-wide distribution and include the nettle-tree butterfly from Europe. They are commonly called the snouts, a name they get from the well-developed labial palps which extend out in front of the head in the form of a snout. Although most of the species are recognised by this characteristic there are other nymphalid butterflies which also have snouts as long as those of the present group, so care should be taken in identifying them in the field. Colourwise, the adults are mainly brown with contrasting paler markings and the outer wing margins are often scalloped. The larvae are smooth, with short hairs, resembling those of the pierids and their main food plants belong to the Ulmaceae.

Sub-family Nymphalinae

What is left of the family Nymphalidae after separation of the other sub-families is included here, though taxonomists doubt that all of the

3,000 species included fit comfortably within the same group. It is, however, possible to recognise within the Nymphalinae a number of major tribes, some of which have been given common names and are therefore identifiable to some extent.

The Argynnini include the fritillaries, with their wings made up of a patchwork of brown, black, yellow and sometimes orange marks. They are butterflies of the northern temperate regions of the world and their larvae tend to be smooth with a forked tail segment and adornments on the head capsule. The Nymphalini include the familiar tortoiseshells, painted ladies, peacock, mourning cloak, red admirals and buckeyes of northern temperate regions. The painted lady butterfly, *Vanessa cardui*, is a migrant and has perhaps the widest distribution of any butterfly in the world. The larvae have a row of spines along the centre of their back as well as a row along each side and they often remain together for several instars after hatching, returning to a silken tent after feeding. Large

Vanessa carye.   The painted lady butterflies are among the most familiar butterflies in temperate zones, and along with the tortoiseshells, peacocks, mourning cloak and red admirals, belong to the sub-family Nymphalini. *Vanessa cardui* is a far-ranging migrant with perhaps the widest distribution of any butterfly in the world. The species pictured is the most colourful and familiar butterfly in Chile, being particularly common in the wetter, temperate south, where the photograph was taken. The butterfly was one of several basking on a patch of grassy waste ground in the middle of the town of Osorno.

Siproeta stelenes meridionalis.   Many tropical nymphalines are particularly
beautiful, this species exhibiting a delicate shade of lime green, a colour rare in
adult butterflies. The species pictured has a wide range, being as common in
Costa Rica as in Peru, where the photograph was taken, in tropical rain forest at
fabulous Tingo Maria.

congregations of the European small tortoiseshell, *Nymphalis urticae*, are a
common sight on nettle leaves in the British Isles. The Limenitini are
the admirals, so-called because of the white banding on the wings, giving
the appearance of the stripes on a naval uniform. (The red admiral also
has striped markings but is a member of the Nymphalini.) Members of
this tribe come from the whole of the American continent, Europe and
Asia. The larvae usually lack the dorsal spines, the median rows only
being present. The remainder of the sub-family contains many colourful
and interesting species of butterflies from all around the world, too
numerous to discuss in detail, though representatives of these will appear
at times in later chapters whenever they have interesting and unusual
characteristics. As a whole, the larvae of the Nymphalinae feed upon a
broad spectrum of plant families.

Chapter 2
Structure of the Adult Butterfly

External features

This chapter deals with the structure and physiology of the adult butterfly with details of the other stages in the life-cycle in the next chapter. The adult butterfly, in common with other insects such as beetles, bugs and grasshoppers, has an external skeleton made from chitin. This exoskeleton consists of plates forming the body segments and tubes forming the appendages. Thinner chitinous membranes in between allow the whole thing to be reasonably flexible. All of the body musculature is found within the exoskeleton, along with the internal organs, which will be described later. The body is sub-divided into the head, thorax and abdomen, all of which bear external appendages of some kind, the whole lot being covered in scales and hairs.

Visible at first glance on the head of a typical butterfly are the two compound eyes, the twin antennae and, during feeding, the proboscis, though this is less noticeable when not in use, being rolled up beneath the head. Also fairly obvious are the labial palps, one on either side of the proboscis, which are concerned with the insect's sense of taste. The proboscis and labial palps are all that remain of the more familiar chewing mouthparts of insects such as locusts and beetles.

The thorax consists of three segments, the prothorax, mesothorax and metathorax, the former having the head joined to it by means of the flexible neck. Each thoracic segment carries a pair of legs, while the meso- and metathorax carry, in addition, a pair of wings. The legs have the usual insect structure with divisions into coxa, trochanter, femur and tibia, with a five-segmented tarsus ending in a pair of claws. In some butterfly families the front legs show considerable structural reduction so that they cannot be used for locomotion. This modification may be restricted to the male alone or may be true of both sexes. The front tibiae are relatively short in most butterflies and in some species they bear, on their inner surface, a spur or epiphysis used for cleaning the antennae. The wings consist of flat, thin, plate-like extensions of the exoskeleton, strengthened by means of hollow, chitinous tubes usually referred to as veins. The arrangement of these veins varies between butterfly families so that the major ones are named and/or numbered as an aid to identification. The movements achieved by butterfly wings are highly com-

Clearly visible in this picture of the nymphalid *Euphaedra neophron* is one of the two compound eyes and the long tubular proboscis. The butterfly is feeding on a fallen doum palm fruit whose tough outer skin, although damaged in this instance, would seem to have little attraction for butterflies. Nevertheless five specimens of this species were feeding, in forest at Mtwapa, near Mombasa, Kenya.

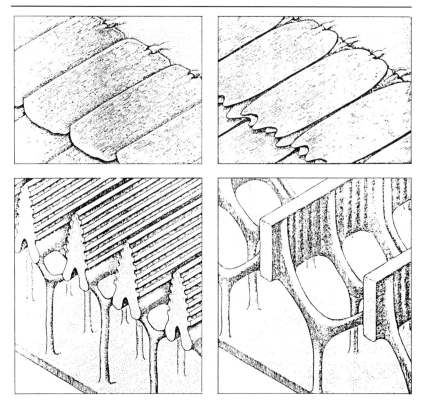

Fig. 1   Two different types of wing scale from a male morpho butterfly. The left-hand scales are taken from the upper wing surface and the fine structure shows the series of ridges which produce the iridescent blue interference colours typical of many species of morpho. On the right are the lower wing scales, with the higher magnification diagram showing the structures which contain the brown pigment.

plex and there is an accordingly complex articulation between the bases of the wings and the thoracic segments which bear them.

Covering both wing surfaces are the scales so typical of the Lepidoptera, each of which has developed as a flattened outgrowth from a single cell. Each scale is about 100 micrometers long by about 50 micrometers in width and their density varies from around 200–600 per square mm. In some of the Acraeinae and Ithomiinae they may be absent from large areas of the wing, revealing the transparent membranes beneath. The transparency of the wing membranes may also be revealed when a butterfly is handled carelessly and the layers of scales are rubbed off, at the same time removing the colour pattern from the wing. Close microscopic examination of the scales shows that the colour patterns are formed from a mosaic of individual scales, each of which has only a single colour. Any particular wing pattern typically consists of only a few colours, three, four or five being usual, and variations in shade and intensity are attained by the mixing of differing proportions of each type of scale. Even greater variation is produced by having varying amounts of any one pigment in the scales and by some scales lacking actual pigment altogether. The perceived colour of the latter is due to the reflection of light from tiny bubbles inside the scales and they are typically found as the white centre of 'eyespots'.

The total number of different pigments involved in the production of all of the beautiful colour patterns in butterflies is relatively small. The majority of them are, for instance, due to melanins. Some of the most fantastic butterfly colours, however, are not a result of pigmentation at all but are due to the structure of the scale surface. These colours are produced by the diffraction (scattering) of or interference with the light falling onto the scales and they appear as iridescent or metallic hues which often change in intensity as the insect moves its wings. This is most strikingly demonstrated in butterflies such as the male morpho whose blue wings seem to appear and then disappear as he flaps lazily around a jungle clearing, this illusion depending upon the angle at which the sunlight strikes the wings. Scattered amongst the other scales, in male butterflies only, are special scent scales whose function will be dealt with later.

Externally, the abdomen appears relatively simple in structure when compared with the head and thorax. It consists of ten segments, the first of which is much reduced in size. The remaining segments appear fairly uniform in size and structure, except for the ninth and tenth segments, which are highly modified as part of the reproductive system. In the male there is a pair of claspers, used to hold the female during mating, and in the female these terminal abdominal segments may be modified to serve as a retractile ovipositor.

The digestive system and feeding

The digestive system and mouthparts of butterflies are adapted for feeding upon a purely liquid diet. This mainly takes the form of nectar from flowers but some butterflies feed on rotting fruits, bird droppings, urine and, in some of the heliconiines, pollen. The latter, however, do not actually eat the pollen, but instead mix it with nectar and then suck up the resulting solution of sugars, amino-acids and other nutrients. In order to make use of this liquid diet the mouthparts of the butterfly are modified to form a tubular, retractile proboscis. When not in use this lies coiled up tightly beneath the head but it can be greatly extended, possibly by means of blood pressure, enabling it to reach down to the nectaries at the base of the petals of the flowers on which it feeds. The flexible tube is actually evolved from the maxillae of the biting insects, the larger mandibles being completely absent in butterflies. Each maxilla consists of a channel and the two are held together to form a single tube by means of interlocking hooks and spines. Running down inside each

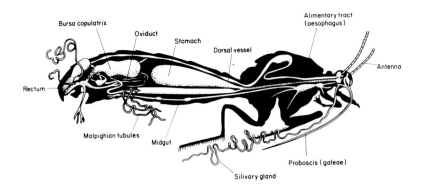

Fig. 2   The internal structure of the adult butterfly.

hollow maxilla is a trachea from the breathing system, a nerve and two sets of diagonally arranged muscles used in coiling the proboscis.

The action of the butterfly proboscis is very much like that of a human sucking a drink through a straw. The pharynx is spherical and its size can be changed by action of the cibarial dilator muscles. These muscles are attached to the outer wall of the pharynx from where they run to a firm attachment on the inside of the tough head capsule. By pulling outwards on the pharynx, they create a reduced pressure inside, which draws liquid up through the proboscis. Muscles in the wall of the pharynx then contract to force the liquid on along the alimentary canal. There would, of course, be a tendency for liquid to be forced back down the proboscis but this is prevented by the presence of a non-return valve which closes the tube. The food may then be stored in the crop or it may pass straight on into the stomach, where digestion and absorption takes place.

It is only in this region of the mid-gut that these processes can proceed for the fore- and hind-guts are lined with impermeable chitin. A proportion of the absorbed food is converted into fat and stored in the fat body where, especially in the female, it may be used later during reproduction. In those butterflies which hibernate, it is the fat body, developed when ample food is available during the summer, which is used to carry them through the winter. The hind gut consists of a coiled ileum, a colon and a short but muscular rectum which stores the faeces before they are voided from the body. Associated with the digestive system, and emptying into the fore-gut in the region of the pharynx, are the salivary glands which, in the Lepidoptera, take the form of long, filamentous tubes lying within the thorax.

The blood circulation

The blood system of the adult butterfly is basically similar to that of all

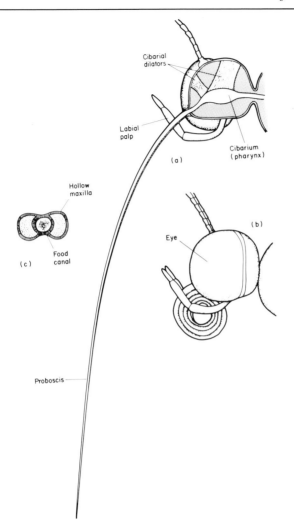

Cibarial
dilators

Labial
palp

Cibarium
(pharynx)

(a)

Hollow
maxilla

(b)

Eye

Food
(c) canal

Proboscis

Fig. 3   a) Section of a butterfly head to show the extended proboscis and associated sucking apparatus. b) A butterfly head showing the coiled proboscis when not in use. c) Section of the proboscis showing how the two hollow maxillae join to form the sucking tube.

other insect groups. Insects possess what is referred to as an open circulation, that is the blood flows around the organs within the body cavity rather than in arteries and veins as it does in humans. The only obvious circulatory structure is the dorsal vessel which, as its name implies, runs along the dorsal surface from the tail end of the abdomen through the thorax and into the head. That portion of the dorsal vessel which passes through the abdomen serves to pump the blood and is

33

therefore referred to as the heart, the more forward portion being the aorta.

Associated with the aorta in butterflies, and acting independently of the heart, are two accessory pulsatile organs, only one of which appears to be significantly functional. The heart is suspended from the wall of the abdomen by a number of filaments and is made up of several segments or chambers into which open a pair of ostia, one from each side. Blood enters the heart from the body cavity, or haemocoel as it is called, through the ostia and is then pumped forward through the aorta towards the head, the chambers contracting one by one from the rearmost forwards. At each ostium the wall of the heart is arranged to form a valve which prevents the flow of blood back into the dorsal sinus, the last named being the particular region of the haemocoel in which the heart lies. At the head end the blood passes out of the open end of the aorta and then flows freely around the various body organs within the haemocoel. Blood flowing to the extremities of the legs, antennae, proboscis and wings flows through distinct channels before returning by a different route and then making its way back to the dorsal sinus and the heart ready for its next circuit. It is likely that movement of blood around the body is also aided by the movement of the butterfly's body during normal activity.

Unlike the blood of humans, that of insects is not used for the transport of respiratory gases around the body, its main function being to transport food substances and waste products. As a result the blood lacks red cells, but other cells, somewhat similar in structure and function to mammalian white blood cells, are present. These cells are called leucocytes and their function is to help defend the butterfly against attack by invading micro-organisms and generally to clear up debris from worn-out or damaged cells.

Breathing and gas exchange

Butterflies, like the majority of insects, breathe by means of a tracheal system. This basically consists of a mass of tubes, passing into the body from the exterior, the finest of which ramify through the organs and the various appendages. Entry to the system from the atmosphere is through openings called spiracles in the sides of the thorax and abdomen. There are nine pairs of spiracles in butterflies, two on the thorax and the remaining seven on the abdomen. The spiracles open into the main trunks of the tracheal system and from these run branching systems eventually ending up in the very fine tracheoles which pass amongst the cells of the various organs.

The main tracheae and the tracheoles are supported by rings of chitin which keep them open at all times. Although passage of air through the main tracheal trunks is aided by pumping movements of the abdomen, actual movement of oxygen to the tissues is by diffusion along the finely branching tracheoles. This is necessarily slow and rather inefficient and is one of the factors which limits the maximum size to which the butterflies have evolved. Some of the carbon dioxide produced passes along the tracheoles in the opposite direction and out of the body through the spiracles, but a proportion of it follows a different route by diffusing directly out through the exoskeleton.

The excretory system

This again is typically insect in design and consists of six blind-ended Malpighian tubules which open into the gut at the junction between the mid- and hind-guts. Each tubule floats freely within the haemocoel, though it is somewhat restrained by its fine covering of respiratory tracheoles. Waste products circulating in the blood are absorbed by the tubular epithelial cells and from there they pass into the tubule lumen before being passed into the gut and finally out through the anus.

The reproductive system

Male butterflies have two testes which may either be separate or, more commonly, fused together as a single structure. They are situated in a dorsal position in the abdomen in segments five and six. From each testis runs a tube called the vas deferens and this eventually widens out to form a seminal vesicle. The seminal vesicles act as sites for the storage of sperm and each vas deferens receives a filamentous accessory gland which probably also serves the same function. The vasa deferentia unite to form a common ejaculatory duct which ends in the aedeagus, the equivalent of the penis. In the female there are two ovaries, both consisting of a number of ovarioles, which empty into a common oviduct having an opening outside the insect on segment nine of the abdomen. Half-way along the oviduct a narrow tube runs to the receptaculum seminis, which holds the sperm following mating and until egg-laying takes place. Opposite and on the ventral surface of the oviduct, another even finer tube runs to a structure, the bursa copulatrix, which has an opening to the outside on segment eight. During mating the sperm from the male is passed into the bursa copulatrix and from here makes its way through these fine tubes and into the receptaculum seminis. As the eggs pass down the oviduct during the laying process, sperms from the receptaculum seminis swim out and fertilise them.

The nervous system

The nervous system of butterflies is much like that of other insects. The central nervous system is represented by a ventral nerve cord running beneath the alimentary canal for most of its length. At intervals along this are concentrations of nerve cells called ganglia and there are usually two of these in the thorax and four in the abdomen. The most prominent ganglion, however, is situated in the head above the pharynx and is usually referred to as the brain. Round either side of the pharynx runs a connection from the brain to the ventral nerve cord. Running from the central nervous system is the peripheral nervous system serving all parts of the butterfly body.

Butterfly sense organs

The most obvious sense organs, as such, on the butterfly are of course the compound eyes, so called because each is composed of a large number of independent visual elements called ommatidia. In the Lepidoptera there may be as many as 17,000 of these ommatidia in a single compound eye. Butterflies possess what is referred to as a eucone type of ommatidium, and these function in the following way. Light rays, parallel with the long axis of the ommatidium, pass through the corneal lens and crystalline cone and impinge upon the light-sensitive retinula. This is connected to a nerve through which a message can be sent to the brain. Light rays passing into the ommatidium at an angle to the long axis are absorbed by pigment in the iris cells. Since each ommatidium is arranged at a slight angle to each of its neighbours, it receives light from only a small area of what is being observed and in this way the butterfly is able to make up a mosaic image of the subject. The general opinion of biologists is that this type of eye is very good at detecting movement, very important in a creature as vulnerable to predation as a butterfly. Since the clarity of the image increases with an increase in ommatidia numbers, it is likely that butterflies can form quite sharp images, at least when compared with other insects with fewer ommatidia. When compared with humans, however, their visual resolution is extremely poor and it is unlikely that they are able to make out the pattern on the wings of another butterfly unless it is very close.

Though the visual acuity of butterflies may not be as good as that of humans, they do have a better range of colour vision, being able to detect colours from ultra-violet through to the red end of the spectrum, in fact the broadest visible spectrum as yet known to exist in the animal kingdom. Although colour vision in butterflies is by no means fully understood, it is likely that in at least some species there may be as many as four different types of colour receptor in the eye in order to cover this broad spectrum of vision. In comparison humans possess only three different types of colour receptor in their retinas.

Butterfly flight

Butterflies have, in general, a greater area of wing in relation to their bodies than any other type of insect and accordingly there are certain aspects of their flight which are unique to them. Whereas most insects use direct flight or else hover, very few of them employ the 'flap and glide' technique of many butterflies and, incidentally, of quite a number of birds. There is, however, a major difference between the birds and the butterflies with regard to flapping and gliding and this relates to the profiles of their respective wings.

In order to glide successfully the profile of the wing needs, ideally, to be that of the typical aerofoil, used by man in the design of aircraft wings and true in general of the wings of most birds. This gives a very high ratio of lift to drag and, accordingly, it reduces the rate of descent under free fall. Research has shown that the butterfly wing is not a good aerofoil, since it has a low ratio of lift to drag, yet undoubtedly butterflies are good gliders. The answer to this apparent paradox is that the surface area of the wing is also of importance when considering gliding ability, and butterflies, as has already been said, have very large wings in relation to their body size. It transpires, in fact, that butterflies parachute-glide through the air, this being due to the way in which they hold their wings to create a concave under-surface, just like a parachute. Now although the wing has a very low lift-to-drag ratio, this in itself slows down the rate of descent as the butterfly glides forwards.

Flapping flight in butterflies is considerably more complex for they have been found to employ a pattern of wing movement unique amongst flying organisms. Analysis of the flight patterns of birds, bats and insects other than butterflies, using high speed cine work, shows that, in all instances, when hovering the tip of the wing follows a basically figure of eight shape in the horizontal plane, though the rest of the wing may simultaneously undergo complex flexing movements. What is so different about the butterflies is that their wings move in a vertical plane during flight and the consequence of this is that they do not follow the well-established norms of aerofoil flight. This unique flight pattern is almost certainly tied up with the fact that butterflies differ somewhat from other insects in the number and arrangement of the wing veins. They tend to have fewer veins than other insects, especially towards the extremities of the wings and there are few cross veins between the main veins which radiate from the wing base. The vein running along the leading edge is the stiffest, a fact obvious to anyone who looks closely at a wing from a dead butterfly. Thus it can be seen that this arrangement means that the butterfly wing has considerable flexibility at the extremities and can also curve easily from front to back. With this set-up in mind, it is now possible to have a look at the wing cycle when a butterfly is hovering, for this is the basis of the type of wing movement involved in the normal, rather lazy flapping flight of most butterflies.

The driving stroke for the flapping flight starts with the wings held together vertically above the body. The wings now begin to move downwards with the leading edges peeling away from each other first and this peeling movement then passes backwards along the wings until it reaches the trailing edges and the wings separate. The wings now move rapidly downwards and, with the pressure below them higher than the pressure above, lift is produced. Due to the fact that, at the same time, the wings are angled to move slightly backwards, forward motion is also achieved. The circulation of air which has been created around the rapidly descending wings is finally shed as a vortex below their tips as they almost meet below the body. The wings are now moved upwards ready for the next downwards power stroke.

37

Chapter 3
The Life-cycle of the Butterfly

The butterflies ae included in what is considered to be the more advanced of the two major sub-divisions of the insects, the Endopterygota. The main characteristic of this group is that they have a life-cycle including a larva and a pupa, though of course all insects start from an egg. The adult butterfly has already been discussed in detail in the previous chapter and the intention here is to consider the egg, larval and pupal stages only, with a brief discussion of the emergence of the adult from the pupa. Egg laying will be dealt with in the following chapter.

The egg

The eggs are formed within the ovarioles of the two ovaries. Each egg starts its development at the blind end of the ovariole and it then grows and matures as it passes towards the oviduct end. The eggs are always orientated within the ovarioles so that the so-called cephalic end of the egg points towards the head end of the parent. The nucleus of the unfertilised egg is surrounded by protoplasm which is filled with tiny spheres of yolk and fat which will nourish the developing larva. During maturation the nucleus moves towards the periphery of the egg where it undergoes division to form an egg nucleus and a number of polar bodies. Around the oocyte, as it is now called, the wall of the ovariole secretes the egg shell or chorion before the fully developed egg moves into the oviduct prior to fertilisation and laying. The chorion is a highly impermeable structure and accordingly there is, in each egg, a micropyle which provides a route for the entry of the sperm to facilitate fertilisation of the ovum, this also permitting gas exchange between the egg and the atmosphere.

Fertilisation of the ovum takes place as the eggs move down the oviduct and past the opening into the receptaculum seminis. The eggs are then usually laid on or very close to the larval food plant although in some species the eggs are scattered while the female is in flight. The eggs themselves differ somewhat in appearance and colour between butterfly species. They vary in shape from that of a spindle to that of a doughnut without the hole, and on the shell there may often be seen a pattern which is a reflection of the surface of the cells lining the ovariole which secreted it. Butterfly eggs are usually of one colour – those of the large white, for instance, are pale yellow – although the overall colour of the egg may appear to change as the larva nears the end of its development and becomes visible through the shell. When it is ready to hatch, the larva bites its way out of the shell and then, depending upon its species, it may eat the remains of the shell, or it may ignore these and immediately start consuming the food plant. This consumption of the shell by some larvae clearly provides them with certain essential nutrients, for if they are prevented from so doing, they fail to survive, even in the presence of adequate amounts of the food plant.

The larva

The body of the larva, or caterpillar as it is more commonly called, is like that of the adult, divided into head, thorax and abdomen. Unlike the adult, the caterpillar does not feed on liquids, and instead of a proboscis the tough head capsule bears a set of strong biting mouthparts. These basically consist of a pair of powerful mandibles with which the caterpillar bites off pieces of leaf, and a pair of maxillae which help to shred the

Eggs of the large white *Pieris brassicae* are placed in batches on plants of Brassicaceae, such as cabbage, as here in the UK. They are normally yellow with finely sculpted surfaces.

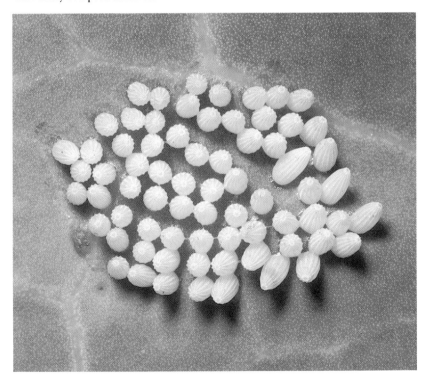

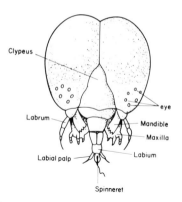

Fig. 4   The structures on the head capsule of a typical caterpillar.

food into smaller pieces before it is swallowed. The underside of the mouth is formed by what might be called a lower lip, the labium, and both this and the maxillae bear small jointed appendages called palps which are used to test the palatability of the food plant. The compound eyes of the adult are absent from the caterpillar which has instead three pairs of simple eyes on either side of the head. Each of these resembles a single unit of the compound eye and it is likely that their sole function is to distinguish between light and dark. This, to some extent, is born out by the way in which some larvae react when a shadow passes over them. A pair of tiny antennae are also present on the front of the head.

The thorax is three-segmented and each segment bears a pair of walking legs. These are five-jointed and their terminal segment, the tarsus, carries a single claw. The abdomen is ten-segmented and bears five pairs of prolegs or false legs, four pairs on segments three to six and a pair usually called claspers on the last segment. The prolegs are not at all like the true legs on the thorax, being fleshy and conical in shape and capable of retraction. The apex of the leg, the planta, is flat or rounded in shape and attached to its centre is a muscle which allows it to be completely inverted. Since the planta carries a series of hooks or crochets, inversion as described helps these to grip onto the surface on which the caterpillar is moving. The way in which the crochets are arranged varies from group to group of the butterflies and is therefore an aid to larval classification.

Internally the caterpillar has the same systems as those found in the adult, with minor differences in arrangement. The alimentary canal runs almost straight from mouth to anus. The largest structure along it is the muscular stomach, which has of course to cope with the great volume of plant food consumed daily by the caterpillar. Saliva is produced by a pair of mandibular glands which lie on either side of the alimentary canal in the thorax. Saliva is secreted onto the food through a pore at the base of each mandible. The nervous, excretory and blood systems are like those of the adult as is the tracheal system, though this does lack the air sacs found in the butterfly. To supply the tracheal system with air there are eight pairs of spiracles on the first eight abdominal segments and one pair on the thorax. The reproductive system is only rudimentary in the caterpillar, though it does begin to show a certain amount of development as the larva grows and progresses through its series of moults.

One aspect of the life of the caterpillar which is absent from the adult is the production of silk, which it uses at the time of pupation. Silk is produced by a pair of glands which lie alongside the alimentary canal and they are, in fact, modified salivary glands. At the head end each gland forms a duct and the two ducts then unite and open to the outside through a structure called the spinneret on the front margin of the labium. Each silk gland consists of a single layer of very large secretory cells surrounding the cavity into which they secrete the silk. During the spinning process the fluid silk passes into a muscular structure, the thread press, which then forces it into the directing tube. Both of these structures are found within the spinneret and the silk emerges from two holes in the directing tube in the form of a double ribbon. Associated with the silk glands is usually a further pair of glands whose secretion helps to harden the silk as it emerges from the spinneret, at the same time helping the two ribbons to adhere to each other.

The basic function of the caterpillar is to feed voraciously and to grow as quickly as possible. Since the insect cuticle which forms the exoskeleton has a limited ability to stretch, growth has to take place by means of a series of moults, during which a new cuticle is formed. This is then inflated so that it will accommodate the tissue formed during the following feeding phase. The factors which initiate moulting are fairly complex but, basically, once the larva reaches a certain size, its brain causes a gland to start the secretion of the moulting hormone ecdysone, a name derived from the alternative word for moulting, which is ecdysis.

Before the old cuticle can be cast off, a new one has to be produced beneath it. The production of this new cuticle is carried out by the epidermal cells, the innermost layer of the caterpillar's exoskeleton. The

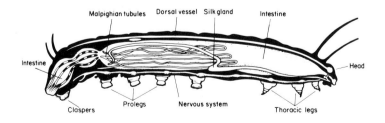

Fig. 5   The internal structure of a caterpillar.

loss of the whole of the old cuticle would represent a significant waste of the caterpillar's body resources, so a considerable amount of recycling takes place at the time that the new one is being formed. The newly forming cuticle secretes protein- and chitin-digesting enzymes which break down the central layers of the old cuticle. This leaves both the outer layer intact to protect the caterpillar and the inner layer intact to prevent digestion of the very cells which secrete the enzymes. It has been shown for insects other than butterflies that as much as 86 per cent of the old cuticle may be resorbed and recycled during this process.

Once the caterpillar is ready to shed its old cuticle, it stops feeding and often positions itself head-down. It then begins to contract the abdominal muscles, raising the pressure in the fluid-filled body cavity, with the result that the old cuticle suddenly splits along a predetermined line of weakness along the back of the thorax. The head end then emerges through this slit and the caterpillar wriggles its way out of the remains of the exuviae, as the old cuticle is called. The caterpillar now swallows air to stretch its body to the size of the new cuticle before it hardens. The number of moults between one larval stage, or instar, and the pupal stage is controlled by a secretion from a small gland, the corpus allatum. This produces juvenile hormone and, as long as it is active, one caterpillar stage follows another until finally, in the fifth instar, the corpus allatum becomes inactive and the caterpillar moults into the pupal stage.

The soft-bodied butterfly caterpillar is, of course, a very vulnerable creature and consequently it has evolved a number of strategies to minimise its chances of becoming an easy meal for some bird or other creature. The number of devices evolved by caterpillars to fool, frighten, sting or poison predators is large and is of such great interest that it is dealt with in detail in Chapter 6. There is, however, one aspect of the butterfly's life which concerns the larvae alone and that is the relationship that some of them have formed with ants, for many of them have come to rely in interesting and even bizarre ways upon their insect relatives. Indeed, of the documented life histories of lycaenid larvae, around 30 per cent were found to be closely associated with ants and it seems likely that this relationship has been vital to the considerable success of the lycaenids as a group.

Perhaps the best known and studied of these relationships is that between caterpillars of the European large blue butterfly, *Maculinea arion*, and ants of the genus *Myrmica*. The female butterfly lays her eggs on the flowers of wild thyme, *Thymus serpyllum*, and the first two larval instars then feed upon the flowers. The third instar bears glands producing sugary secretions and these attract ants to tend and presumably defend it against attack from insect enemies. Following the next moult, the fourth instar caterpillar leaves the food plant and climbs down to the ground. It then arches its back and, by secreting chemical messengers called pheromones, it induces a *Myrmica* ant to seize it in its jaws and carry it down into the latter's nest. Here, the caterpillar feeds upon ant larvae until, in May, having overwintered in the ants' nest, it pupates.

The slug-like larva of this species of *Narathura* butterfly, a lycaenid,
is accompanied by a protective squad of fierce green tree ants, *Oecophylla
smaragdina*, which are irresistibly attracted to a sweet substance secreted by the
larva. The ants are pugnaciously defensive of the larva, keeping parasites and
other enemies at bay, even jumping onto the photographer's hands as they
frantically attempt to keep him away. Photographed in tropical rain forest near
Cairns in Queensland, Australia.

This unusual story is concluded when the adult butterfly emerges from
its underground pupa and makes its way to the surface, protected once
again from the ants' possible attack by some appeasing secretion. Once
out in the open it seeks out a suitable perch in order to inflate and
harden its wings before it eventually takes flight.

An alternative strategy for making use of ants and appeasing their
carnivorous appetite has been evolved by a number of lycaenid larvae.
By producing a sugary secretion which is irresistibly attractive to ants,
they can gain access to herds of aphids tended by ants, on a kind of
'honorary membership' basis. Ants are normally fiercely protective towards their aphid herds, ferociously attacking intruders both large and
small, and any caterpillar which comes their way is likely to end up as a
meal. However, by indulging the ant's sweet tooth, the lycaenid larvae
are actively encouraged and protected by the ants, who remain seemingly oblivious to the inroads made by the rapidly growing caterpillars as
they munch their way through the bucking herds of aphids. It seems
likely that the ants do not do so badly out of this arrangement for they
glean significant quantities of amino acids and sugars from the caterpillar's secretions. The caterpillar achieves a considerable gain from the
system by securing access to a protein-rich diet which would otherwise
be inaccessible. On the debit side, it only has to allocate a small proportion of its rich dietary intake to the manufacture of the ants' reward. No
system, however, consists entirely of winners and here it is the aphids
who are the all-round losers.

Other lycaenid larvae simply exploit many ants' cravings for sweetness by recruiting them as voluntary and willing guardians who efficiently drive off predators and parasitoids while the caterpillars browse in comparative safety on their food plant. This protection may also extend to pupae, some of which continue to secrete the anti-appeasement substance, thus ensuring that a platoon of ant guards is on constant watch over them. The lycaenid *Jalmenus evagoras* in Queensland, Australia is tended by several species of quite large and aggressive *Iridiomyrmex* ants. These are highly effective pickets against intruding spiders, wasps, parasitoids and other ants, mortal enemies of the caterpillars and immune to their inveigling secretions. Also in Queensland I have, on a number of occasions, found larvae of a *Narathura* species of lycaenid accompanied by a protective squad of green tree ants, *Oecophylla smaragdina*. Up to a dozen of these fairly large ants were present at one time, walking over the caterpillar and gently caressing its surface with their mandibles in a constant quest for sugary satiety. My close approach with the camera triggered a frantic response from these alert guardians, who started to dash wildly around in a vigorous attempt to take on allcomers. Some even mounted a pre-emptive assault, actually jumping the short distance onto my hand and attacking me physically and, fortunately in this species, painlessly. With this kind of response it is not surprising that the ants form an effective garrison in defence of the butterfly caterpillars. Similarly, in Trinidad I have seen gregarious lycaenid larvae clad in a living robe of tiny, rust-coloured ants, which were capable of mounting a surprisingly painful attack upon unprotected human skin. They constantly fussed around on the glistening backs of the larvae, presenting a formidable animated blockade against any would-be aggressors, with up to 40 ants on each larva at any one time.

In the next stage of development there is an unusual and interesting defence employed by certain blues and metalmarks, again related to ants. This is the ability of their pupae to produce audible or ultrasonic sounds which are believed to be of advantage to them in two possible ways. One is that the sounds encourage accompanying ants to attack parasitoids which are attempting to lay their eggs in the pupae. Secondly, it is thought that the sounds produced may warn off bird or mammalian predators which have previously had unpleasant encounters with the ants aroused by the pupae.

The pupa

When the final instar is fully grown it seeks out a place to undergo the transformation from caterpillar to pupa, or chrysalis as it is often called in the butterflies. Pupation may take place in a variety of situations depending upon the species concerned. Some pupate in silk-lined cocoons in the soil, others behind bark or in other concealed situations, whilst some of them may do so in fully exposed positions. The first indication that the caterpillar is ready to pupate is when it stops feeding and the contents of the alimentary canal are expelled. As the pupal cuticle is being formed beneath the larval cuticle, the characteristic colour of the latter is usually lost and it becomes darker and somewhat wrinkled.

Precisely what happens next depends upon the pupation site, but it is at this point in the butterfly life-cycle that the silk glands come into use. For those butterflies in which pupation takes place in the soil, the process is fairly straightforward. The excavation is first lined with silk to form the cocoon and the larva then undergoes a moult very similar to that between instars, the pupa breaking out of the old cuticle and finally wriggling its way free of the exuviae, which remains with it in the cocoon. At first the pupa is pale in colour but with exposure to the air the pupal cuticle soon hardens and adopts its final coloration. For those species which pupate above ground the strategy is somewhat different and results in one of two different arrangements. In both instances, the caterpillar first weaves a silken pad which it holds onto by means of the crochets on the abdominal claspers. It may then sit in a head-up position

Attached by a silken pad, the final instar caterpillar of a comma butterfly
Polygonia c-album hangs in an inverted position as it waits to begin the change into
a pupa. Photographed in the UK.

and weave a silken girdle, or it may hang in an inverted position. In
both instances, the old cuticle now splits and the pupa begins to wriggle
its way out of the exuviae, which is gradually worked backwards until it
is almost free of the rear end. At this point the pupa is still holding on to
the exuviae by its tail end, but it now has to perform a very delicate
manoeuvre in order to become completely free of the old cuticle. On the
final abdominal segment is a hooked process, the cremaster, and as this
comes free of the exuviae, it is pushed out onto the silk pad into which
the hooks are worked. The rear end of the pupa now releases its hold on
the exuviae, which drops away to the ground below. The pupae are pale
in colour at this stage, but, as with those already described above, they
soon harden and darken to their final colour.

In appearance, the pupa probably resembles the adult butterfly more
than it does the caterpillar which gave rise to it. Externally, head, thorax
and abdomen are clearly defined and the positions of adult structures,
such as the proboscis, antennae, legs and wings, can clearly be made out.
The spiracles show the same arrangement as that of the caterpillar
except that the last abdominal pair is non-functional. Internally, great
changes take place in the pupa in the transformation from the caterpillar
to the adult arrangement, a process referred to as metamorphosis.

These changes are very complex in nature but basically involve a
breakdown and rebuilding of most of the organ systems and, of course,
the development of the adult structures already mentioned as being
visible externally on the pupa. The alimentary canal is non-functional
during this time and the anus is blocked off. Consequently there is also
no loss of excretory products which are stored instead within the developing hind gut. Being unable to feed, the pupa cannot take in any
water either and, as a consequence, the cuticle is covered in a layer of
wax to reduce water loss. During the pupal phase the butterfly is
completely motionless, although as the new abdominal muscles begin to
develop, violent movements of the abdomen may be initiated if it is
threatened in any way.

The duration of the pupal stage varies from a few days in many
tropical species to months or sometimes a year or more in those butterflies whose pupae undergo a period of diapause. The phenomenon of
diapause is common in many insects and represents a period of suspended animation which allows them to get through a time of climatic
extreme such as winter or a drought. As a consequence, diapause tends
to be found in temperate butterflies which overwinter as pupae or in
butterflies of desert habitats, where absence of rain means absence of the
larval food plant. In temperate species of butterfly with more than one
generation per year, only the autumn-produced pupae undergo diapause. It has been found that there are some differences between diapause and non-diapause pupae of the same species. It was found, for

instance, that in four species of Japanese white butterflies, the diapause pupa had a thicker layer of wax covering the cuticle, presumably to act both as an insulator and to reduce water loss over the long resting period.

The pupal stage is probably less vulnerable to attack than the caterpillar, since it is movement which tends to attract predatory animals such as birds and the pupa remains immobile for most of its existence. Those pupae which remain beneath the soil or are carefully hidden are, of course, less vulnerable than those which remain in full view and it is in the latter that we find camouflaged forms which are described in detail in Chapter 6.

The emergence of the adult butterfly

Once development is complete and external conditions are suitable, the adult butterfly will emerge from the pupa. Emergence of the adult, referred to as eclosion, follows much the same pattern as that of the various instars from their cuticles and the pupa from its skin. Initially, the pupa splits along the line of weakness on top of the thorax and the head, antennae and legs are carefully extracted. The butterfly usually then takes a short rest before extracting its abdomen from the pupal skin. For those butterflies in which the pupa was contained in a cocoon, the next task is to escape from it. This may be done either by mechanical means, the adult cutting its way out, or by the production of secretions which soften the silk. The newly emerged adult must now very quickly find a suitable place to hang, tail downwards, so that it can inflate its crumpled wings. At this stage the wings are very soft and by pumping blood under pressure into the wing veins, they slowly expand to their full size. The butterfly now sits for a while, occasionally flapping its wings, uncoiling and coiling its proboscis and flexing its legs while the cuticle dries out and hardens. At this juncture the uric acid stored up during the remodelling process within the pupa is excreted in the form of a liquid, usually reddish in colour, called the meconium. Once this process is complete the butterfly is able to fly off and assume the life of an adult.

Chapter 4
Adult Behaviour – Courtship and Reproduction

Considering the length of time during which the capturing and collecting of butterflies has been popular, remarkably little detailed research has been carried out on their actual courtship behaviour and even casual observations are relatively few in number. For detailed observations and analyses we are still heavily dependent on the work of a small handful of workers, often from many years ago.

As with most other animals, it is the male butterflies which are normally the active sex in initiating mating, although the females of certain species may play a part in soliciting sexual contact. Butterfly males can broadly be divided into two types. In the first of these the male actively patrols up and down a certain area or 'beat', along a hedgerow, woodland ride or jungle river where females may be feeding on flowers or laying eggs from a previous mating. The European orange-tip, *Anthocharis cardamines*, is a typical example of a patrolling butterfly. The males are most commonly observed flying rapidly, with a lilting motion, along a hedgerow, darting briefly downwards to examine a likely leaf or flower which resembles the pale-coloured female. Every now and then he may stop briefly to refuel, often on the flowers of the larval food plant.

The second strategy employed by male butterflies involves the establishment of a territory. This is defended vigorously against intruding males of its own as well as other species and in fact any object which crosses his invisible frontier will be closely investigated, including other insects, falling leaves and even curious humans. I well remember, while walking through a patch of forest in the Shimba Hills in Kenya, the heart-stopping surprise of having the large and powerful flying male of the nymphalid *Euxanthe tiberius* come so close as actually to brush my face when I invaded his territory. Having investigated me closely, he returned to his perch on a tree trunk on the edge of a sunlit glade. (I would like to point out at this juncture, to those armchair lepidopterists amused at my easy shockability, that in Africa things which suddenly come down from trees and touch your face can be deadly.) This particular male proved excessively sensitive to nearby movements, several times darting out to investigate passing insects but always returning predictably to within a few centimetres of his original perch on the trunk.

In common with others in the genus the males of *Euxanthe tiberius* establish and defend their territory, in this case a tree in a sunlit spot in the Makadara Forest in the Shimba Hills near Mombasa, Kenya. Males of such powerfully flying species as this will investigate any intruders into their domain, including other butterflies, birds and wildlife photographers.

Males of the amazing Neotropical cracker butterflies in the genus *Hamadryas* seem to warn off other males intruding on their territory by using an audible alarm system. This consists of a cracking sound, produced by the wings, which is surprisingly sharp and penetrating. It is an unforgettable experience to watch a pair of males engaged in an aerial dispute, circling in a dizzy helter-skelter to a staccato accompaniment of quite astounding volume. I observed it for the first time in early September in tropical southern Mexico, at a time when all of the *Hamadryas ferentina* males seemed to be constantly jousting in this way. Since then I have seen numerous other species of the same genus in several other countries, but have seldom heard them again in such strident aerial debate; presumably this behaviour is seasonal and linked to the breeding period.

Territorial behaviour was first noted as long ago as 1902 when N. H. Joy observed that the males of the European purple emperor, *Apatura iris*, would set up a guard-post or 'throne' on the branch of an oak, defending the surrounding airspace from intruding males. Removing the resident male merely resulted in the annexation of the territory, which may extend up to an area of 100 sq m (120 sq yd), by the next male to arrive on the scene. Males of territorial species inhabiting mountainous or hilly areas often establish themselves on the prominent summit of a hill or ridge, thus giving rise to the name of 'hill-topping' butterflies. I well remember an extremely gruelling and sweaty day spent climbing through the lush forests covering the slopes of Trinidad's highest mountain, Mount Tamana. My reward was the briefest glimpse of a splendid black and orange nymphalid *Catonephele numilia* which seemed to be absent from the dense forest lower down but whose males could be reliably spotted swooping vigorously across the bare summit at the centre of their territory. Many male butterflies probably practise at certain times both patrolling and territorial behaviour although even the most sedentary of species will temporarily forsake his watching-brief for feeding purposes.

The way in which holdings are established and defended has been closely studied in the European speckled wood butterfly, *Pararge aegeria*. A resident male defends a patch of sunlit forest floor, which is a fairly scarce commodity beneath the dense canopy of leaves, with the result that other males are constantly arriving and territorial skirmishes are frequent, involving a brief spiralling flight from which the intruder soon breaks away and retreats. The most noticeable aspect of these encounters is their obviously ritualised nature and the fact that the male in residence always seems to win. Squatting rights would therefore appear to be of major significance in this species, perhaps as a means of avoiding an unnecessary amount of physical contact which would result in an unacceptable degree of wing wear and tear. Retreat by the intruder therefore seems to be the wise move as a damage-limitation exercise and, after all, the vanquished male is always in a position to set up a territory on his own account, as sunny spots wax and wane as the sun changes its position in the sky.

Researchers removing a territory-holder to see what happens discovered, not surprisingly, that his place is rapidly taken by a newcomer who, if allowed to gain residential status by being permitted to remain

Male speckled woods, *Pararge aegeria*, a common European satyrine, establish and defend territories in sunlit spots in woodland, driving off intruding males. Photographed in the UK.

for just a few seconds without being disturbed, will proceed to drive off any intruders, including the former owner when he is re-introduced. This establishes that it is not the most 'athletic' or the 'fittest' butterfly which establishes a territory but merely the first to arrive and set up shop in a likely place. Being active early in the day and not being tempted to visit a patch of neighbouring flowers too often would seem to be more desirable attributes for 'success' in a male speckled wood than mere physical prowess. In another experiment two such males were allowed to establish territories in the same area but without actually seeing one another. When removed and then re-introduced in sight of each other, an unusually protracted spiralling contest took place, seemingly spurred on in this artificially created situation by the fact that each butterfly 'knew' that it was the rightful 'owner' and so was 'sure' about the justness of its cause in driving off the 'intruder'.

Males of the speckled wood probably abide in their miniature woodland domains for a number of days until they eventually die. Male small tortoiseshells, *Nymphalis urticae*, on the other hand, are more like the hoboes of the butterfly world, setting up an abode for merely an afternoon or so before moving on. In this species territory is established next to a site likely to attract ovipositing females, usually a patch of nettles, *Urtica dioica*. This will be energetically defended against intruding males until a female comes upon the scene. Territorial defence is then waived in favour of guarding the female, a duty which involves perching closely behind her and tapping her sharply with his antennae at intervals of a few seconds. This strange action is performed with amazing vigour, such that the sound of the clubbed antennae striking the female's hind wings can be heard at a distance of a metre or more. Intruding males are lured away to a 'safe' distance in a mad aerial dash, culminating in the sudden direct return of the resident male to resume his antennal drumming. However, he may well have failed to shake off the other male, who will often put in a further unwelcome appearance, sparking off another round of interactions. Such events may be repeated many times over the course of an afternoon and numerous trespassing males may have to be evicted before the original territory-holder manages to mate with the female, if he is quick enough, before she goes to roost.

Another possible method of establishing an exclusive living-space is exhibited by certain ithomiines, although the actual nature of this activity is currently under discussion. In the shadowy depths of the tropical rain forest, male ithomiines may often be seen perched motionless on a leaf, displaying the fringes situated on the leading edges of the hindwings. It has been found that these wing-edge hairs release a chemical substance which has been identified as containing a lactone. The hypothesis has been put forward that the release of this volatile substance acts as a male territorial-recognition pheromone, designed to warn off intruding males, not only of the same species but also of other species producing lactones. I have seen and photographed this behaviour in the Atlantic coast rainforest reserve at Montes Claros in Minas Geraes State, Brazil.

This male ithomiine, *Mechanitis lysimnia*, is perched with the fringes on the leading edges of its hindwings fully extended. Depending on which of two theories is correct, this butterfly is either releasing a pheromone to warn off intruding males, or releasing a pheromone to attract other males and females of its own and related species to establish a communal mating lek. Perhaps both theories might prove to be correct under different circumstances. The picture was taken in semi-deciduous tropical forest at Fazenda Montes Claros Reserve in Minas Geraes State, Brazil.

Mate recognition

Male butterflies spend only a fleeting period of time on the wing before old age claims them. During their brief lives they must not squander their sole opportunity to pass on to future generations as many of their genes as possible. With the airspace around them crowded with other insects of all kinds a considerable amount of confusion and wasting of precious time would occur without some quick and reliable way of recognising females of their own species. It is equally essential for males of the same species to recognise one another quickly and preferably from a distance, thus avoiding time needlessly frittered away in fruitless male-male courtship or in skirmishing. Butterflies are the supreme examples of day-flying lepidopterans, highly prized for their peerless kaleidoscopic tapestry of wing colour and patterns. It has always been an accepted fact that these colours must play a vital role in sexual recognition and courtship, especially in cases where a brilliant male differs markedly from a drably garbed female. This may not necessarily be the case, however, for it now appears that scent, in the form of specific pheromones, might actually play a role in the sex lives of butterflies, a role almost equal in prominence to that found in their nocturnal brethren the moths.

Charles Darwin was much concerned with the function of the bright wing patterns in butterflies, especially where marked sexual dimorphism was concerned. He felt certain that the brilliant coloration of many male butterflies must have been the result of preferential selection by the females, who would be seduced more easily by the more splendidly coloured of whichever males were suing for her favours. Unfortunately for the survival of this concept, which so conveniently explains much of what we observe in butterfly coloration, it does not appear to stand up to the penetrating gaze of experimental evidence. Successive researchers in this field have asked themselves a number of pertinent questions. What particular segments or aspects of a colour-pattern could be used for visual recognition? Do the sexes conduct their courtship rituals in a way which indicates that they are actually using colour and pattern as an important and integral part of their communication? Is a female's colour-pattern important to a male in recognising and possibly choosing among different females? Do female butterflies consistently spurn one male's advances and yet subsequently succumb to the courtship overtures of another, thus exhibiting apparent discrimination between suitors? If this is the case, is it actually the colours of the respective males which influence the female's 'decision' or is it some other factor?

Appearing to support the theory of the importance of colour in courtship is the amazingly broad spectral range of the butterfly's eye, which reaches into the ultra-violet, a portion of the spectrum which may be more vital to butterfly communication than the gorgeous colours visible to our own spectrally more limited eyes. On the other hand, while their colour perception is acute, their actual image resolution is restricted and it seems probable that butterflies are incapable of resolving a clear and detailed image until an object is extremely close. This represents a visual acuity which is several thousand times less sensitive than our own. Butterflies do have more or less wrap-round vision, coupled with a refined ability to detect movement, and this relates to their capability, superior to our own, of resolving rapidly presented images, the so-called flicker-vision. This would presumably enable them to pick out, much more easily, the essentials of the pattern on the moving wings of another butterfly.

Colour patterns

It seems obvious that the visual faculties of the butterfly described above play a significant role in permitting recognition of colour and patterns, but what of the patterns themselves? It is perhaps ironic that while the splendid colours of so many butterflies have led to their premature demise on the point of a pin, it may be those wavelengths invisible to our eyes which are most important to butterflies. Thus the wings of many species have been proved to reflect or absorb varying amounts of light at the ultra-violet end of the spectrum, providing a kind of private communication line unavailable to their vertebrate predators or their human admirers. It is particularly notable that many species which appear uninspiringly uni-coloured to our eyes in normal light, such as many of the whites, actually exhibit specific and marked patterns in ultra-violet light, which is of course invisible to us. This may be an important factor for patrolling males in their quest for females perched inconspicuously (to our eyes) among vegetation, for leaves generally absorb UV light very strongly. A female sitting in such a position, whose wings are brightly reflecting UV light, would therefore stand out like a beacon to a searching male. Even iridescent species, such as the flashing blue morphos, which appear brilliantly coloured to our eyes, may shine still more intensely in ultra-violet light. By making use of the ultra-violet or the visible spectrum males can obviously recognise sufficient aspects of a female's patterns to home in on her; but what of species such as *Papilio dardanus*, whose females exhibit polymorphism, or males such as those of many species of ithomiines and heliconiines, who themselves are members of intricate mimicry rings? If in these butterflies reliance was placed solely upon visual clues for identification of their own females, then a confused orgy of intraspecific matings would result. That this does not happen very often is evident, so presumably some other clues such as scents must be employed in these cases making this a ripe field for further research.

Courtship

Poorly understood though it may be in our present state of knowledge, it is nevertheless clear that courtship in butterflies is a complicated and ritualised affair relying for its success on the presentation of the correct sequence of stimuli in the visual, tactile and olfactory fields. Putting it more simply, male and female butterflies must usually look, feel and smell right to each other before mating can take place. There are, however, the exceptions to the rule, as has been demonstrated by the male *Colias*, who merely requires the presence of a stationary female-like object to trigger his entire courtship sequence. His mate-identification requirements are, in fact, so simple that he can be satisfied by and will even attempt to copulate with a paper dummy. Despite this it seems for most species that the complete cocktail of stimuli must be mixed in the correct order for mating to proceed. The most thoroughly studied butterfly in this respect is probably the European grayling, *Hipparchia semele*, partly as a result of the classic work of Niko Tinbergen and his colleagues. While individual facets may differ, the following sequence of actions is broadly followed by numerous other butterfly species.

In the grayling the courtship sequence is initiated by the male flying in pursuit of the female, his positive response to her presence having been induced by visual stimuli. These need not be particularly specific, for it can readily be observed that male graylings and males of most other butterflies will set off in hot pursuit not only of other butterflies but also of large bees, falling leaves and birds. By presenting lures of various shapes, sizes and colours researchers have established that the female's colour is not especially important and in fact the males were more excited by red or black lures than by those of the correct female-like shade. Shape was significant and although circular or rectangular lures elicited pursuits as strongly as butterfly-shaped ones, there was definitely a preference for rectangles with sides of similar length over long narrow ones. Size seemed even more enticing, with extra-large lures being followed more readily than female-sized ones, while adding a realistic skipping flight action was more successful than allowing the dummy to take a straight path. These results signified that male graylings rely solely on visual stimuli for continued pursuit of a female.

If the female being pursued is receptive she will eventually fall to the ground, rapidly followed by the male who lands beside her and moves in a semi-circle to face her. Now follows a set routine during which the male initially shivers his wings, then rotates his antennae in broad circles and expands his wing movement to produce a fanning action. Next he lays his antennae on the ground and arches his body, bringing his forewings forward to hood the female's antennae. This is intended to 'stimulate' the female by bringing the sensitive receptors on her antennae into intimate contact with the pheromone (sometimes called 'love dust') secreted by two thin bands of closely spaced androconia on his forewings. The male now edges round and tries to make physical contact with the female's abdomen. A female in receptive condition will raise her wings slightly, exposing her abdomen so that coupling can take place at the first attempt; her refusal is indicated by a rapid opening and closing of the wings.

In the grayling the role of 'love dust' seems only to assume a significant degree of importance during the latter stages of courtship. In other butterflies olfactory clues may actually spark off courtship in the first place and this is especially so in those very members of the Ithomiinae and Heliconiinae for which membership of a mimicry ring complicates visual recognition. The essential part played by olfactory stimuli is discussed in greater detail below, with special reference to male danaine butterflies.

Returning to the grayling, the process of establishing the full copulatory position may take a few seconds and during this time the male can usually be seen making questing movements with the tip of his abdomen in an attempt to interlock with the genitalia of the female. Once established, the bond between the male and female genitalia is very strong and in many species there ensues a post-nuptial flight of the two interlocked butterflies to a place of relative safety, such as deep among grasses or beneath leaves. In graylings, the act of copulation lasts on average around one hour, although, in general, data on the duration of this act in butterflies are scanty. What is known is that in *Danaus gilippus*, whose courtship is described in greater detail below, the average period spent in copulation is seven to eight hours, while in *D. chrysippus* it ranges from just over one hour to as long as twelve hours. This latter species tends to restrict its mating activity to the afternoon and undertakes a post-nuptial flight during which the male carries the female, suspended by his genitalia, to some concealed spot where they can remain in peace until dusk. It is unlikely, therefore, that such a female will mate more than twice in one day. Other butterflies may actually spend the hours of darkness in copulation and I remember once, at 7.30 a.m. in the Shimba Hills in Kenya, discovering a pair of *Acraea ceresa* nestled amongst the grass and glistening in the early morning sunlight with droplets of dew.

There may even be an apparently conscious 'choice' exercised in the selection of an eventual mating site. I have, for example, several times seen the yellow pierid, *Phoebis sennae*, on the edge of tropical forests; each time the insect has been resting quietly among yellowing leaves, closely matching the colour of its undersides and thus rendering it extremely inconspicuous. In Mexico I encountered a mating pair of these butter-flies, but only spotted them at the last moment, too late to prevent their flight away from the jaundiced leaf on which they had been discreetly mating. Refusing to give them up for lost I watched them closely as they circled around the forest clearing, several times dropping down and landing briefly on a leaf, only to resume their flight at the last moment. Finally they selected a spot and settled down, right next to a yellowing leaf which, judging by their behaviour in rejecting other possible sites, they had actually chosen deliberately as a matching, cryptic background.

There is always considerable competition between males for available females and, as a result, most females probably mate more than once during their lifetimes. The long-lived danaine females will lay successive egg-batches fertilised by many different males, a promiscuous life-style which has the benefit of producing a high level of recombination of the genes. Post-copulatory competition from other males of the species is prevented in some butterflies, notably Acraeinae and Parnassiinae, by the male inserting a plug in the female to prevent further matings. Alterna-tively, during copulation in certain heliconiines, the males dust the females with an anti-aphrodisiac, which has been shown to be highly effective in discouraging further courtship by competing males, no mat-ter how ardent they are.

Most of the potential sexual encounters which I have observed be-tween butterflies have proved to be a fruitless endeavour on the part of the male. This is not at all surprising, since most females encountered will have already mated with another male and may be unable or unwilling to do so again. Male butterflies do tend to be very persistent, however, and an unreceptive or apparently 'coy' female may be relent-lessly pursued for some considerable time. The most obvious sign of the female's rejection of the male's overtures is the elevation of her abdomen, thus putting it in a position in which the male cannot couple his genitalia. This is, therefore, an effective method of preventing rape and in mature females the only method by which a male can secure a successful copulation is via a complete courtship which results from her voluntary acquiescence; teneral females, i.e. those which have only re-cently emerged from the pupa may, however, succumb to rape, being unable to prevent it in their delicate condition.

We come now to the thorny question of whether the males and females actually 'choose' each other on the basis of colour and pattern and whether there is really any form of discrimination, with 'prettier' colours

Danaus chrysippus. Plain tiger butterflies, family Nymphalidae: Danainae. Butterflies copulate in a back-to-back position. Once the genitalia are fully engaged the bond is remarkably strong. This species tends to restrict its mating activity to the late afternoon, and undertakes a post-nuptial flight with the female dangling from the male's genitalia, as seen here. They retire to some concealed place where they can remain unmolested until dusk, the actual act of copulation lasting between one and twelve hours. Just visible behind the female's head is the aposematic pupa of the acraeine *Acraea andromacha*. Photographed in marshy woodland on Townsville Common in Queensland, Australia.

Acraea ceresa ceresa, family Nymphalidae: Acraeinae.   Having remained in copula overnight these two butterflies sparkle with dew in the early morning in grassland in the Shimba Hills near Mombasa, Kenya.

being preferred over 'dull' ones. In general all male butterflies are most attracted to objects coloured more or less like their own females; detailed pattern seems to be of little importance as long as the general ground-colour or any conspicuously contrasting colours are reproduced. In addition ultra-violet reflection or absorption by the female's wings is also an essential factor in those species where it is prominent. Movement certainly seems to increase the attractiveness of dummies and in experiments with the silver-washed fritillary, *Argynnis paphia*, such movement was essential in order to hold the male's attention.

If female colour were to play a significant role in the male's location and 'choice' of a mate we could perhaps expect it to be most obviously displayed in species with dimorphic or polymorphic females, i.e. those with two or more distinct colour forms. Experimental evidence to date does, however, indicate a lack of distinct preferences for one colour over another. For example, in the North American tiger swallowtail, *Papilio glaucus*, the males invariably exhibit a kind of tiger-striped pattern, whereas the females may be similarly coloured or else dark, this latter mimicking the unpalatable blue swallowtail, *Battus philenor*. Available evidence suggests that the males mate randomly with both forms, with no preference for either colour form being exhibited. Against this, females of the butterfly *Anartia amathea*, with their usual orange-red colour changed to black, were far less attractive to their males than the normally coloured females. Thus, although female colour is an aid to advertising her presence to a prospecting male, it is unlikely that it does anything more than tell the latter that she is something more than the many other aerial objects, such as other insects, which regularly pass through his field of vision. This lack of any real discrimination on the part of the male is amply demonstrated in the abundant polymorphism displayed by many female butterflies, such as *Papilio dardanus*, where scent instead plays the major role in initiating the full courtship sequence.

As mentioned at the start of this chapter, it has long been a widely held view that by exercising selection female butterflies have been responsible for the bright colours of the males in species where the females tend to be drab and the males colourful, e.g. in many lycaenids having bright blue males and brown females. If the bright colours of most male butterflies really do play a vital sexual role then we should expect experimental evidence to indicate a strong female preference for males of the 'correct' colour. We should also expect vividly coloured young males to be more attractive than older, faded males with tattered wings. Experimental evidence to date does not seem to support this widely held view, which has always so conveniently been used to explain away the flashiness so typical of male butterflies. In experiments with the florid scarlet and black *Anartia amathea*, females were found to be as ready to mate with normally coloured red males as with males painted black all over. The females are perfectly capable of seeing the normal male's startling red colours, which are the most conspicuous element in his pattern and the only bright colour present, so their failure to show the slightest visual discrimination between the two types of male is a severe blow to the 'choice by colour' theory of female preferences.

In another experiment two species of butterflies were employed, *Colias eurytheme*, with orange males having ultra-violet-reflecting wings and *C. philodice*, whose males have yellow, ultra-violet-absorbing wings. The wing colours of the two species were artificially reversed, taking care to maintain the ultra-violet reflection on the wings of the *C. eurytheme* males. Despite the switch, the females of each species still continued to recognise their own males and happily accepted altered males as freely as normal specimens.

In a later experiment the males' colours were changed even more radically, being dyed blue, green, red or orange all over. This whole spectrum of male changelings was accepted just as readily by the females as unaltered males exhibiting the 'correct' colour. Far more important was the ultra-violet reflection on the wings of the *C. eurytheme* males; no matter what their visible (to our eyes) colour, a significant reduction in matings was experienced by males whose ultra-violet reflection had been removed. On the other hand, this absence of any ultra-violet reflection did not suddenly make them acceptable to females of the other species, whose own males have the ultra-violet-absorbing wings. The net result of these fascinating experiments indicates that females of *C. eurytheme* completely ignore the 'visible' colours and are impressed solely by the ultra-violet component in their males' wing coloration. *C. philodice* females, however, act as though hopelessly colour-blind and fail totally to respond either to 'visible colours' or to ultra-violet reflection.

It thus appears likely that the attractive concept that female butterflies 'admire' male colours and choose their mates on this basis may not be correct at all, with the exception of reflection in the ultra-violet. Nevertheless, it is a fact that females do exercise a certain amount of selection, readily showing rejection behaviour when spurning the initial advances of a courting male, though perhaps accepting him after repeated advances on his part. Maybe sheer persistence is an important card in the pack of stimuli employed by the courting male; after all, if a male has the energy to spend several minutes energetically hovering near a female, he must be reasonably 'fit' to fertilise her eggs. This might also explain why it is that a tattered male with washed-out colours can still be a successful suitor. It also seems certain that olfactory stimuli are of supreme importance to the female in choosing a mate and the aspects of this interesting section of butterfly biology will be discussed next.

We have already seen how scent produced by male androconia is important in the courtship of the grayling butterfly and the sole factor in influencing male acceptance by the females of *Colias philodice*. In these and many other species of butterflies, the apparatus producing the scents is inconspicuous or concealed during courtship and it is not always obvious to the observer at which juncture the male is actually actively disseminating scents and evidence of this is frequently circumstancial at best. In the Danainae (and probably Ithomiinae) scent production and dissemination has seemingly reached a high level of sophistication and

Why should the male of the gorgeous *Anartia amathea* flaunt his brilliant scarlet livery when experimental evidence indicates that the females will readily accept males which are black all over? Photographed at the SIMLA Biological Station in Trinidad, where this lovely nymphalid is abundant in the disused cocoa plantation and the garden.

complexity. Observations on these butterflies are aided by the fact that the males are able to switch scent production on and off at will, simply by everting the conspicuous hair pencils at the tip of the abdomen (Danainae) or the fringes at the front margin of the hind wing (Ithomiinae). The androconial organs of the Danainae actually produce particles, in that androconial scales, the pheromone-bearing 'love-dust' mentioned earlier, simply break off at a predetermined point of weakness and are then scattered to the winds by the male. Nearly 100 years ago there were descriptions given of numbers of male *Euploea* circling in large aggregations, scattering androconia from their everted hairpencils in such quantities as to pervade the air with their aroma. Several times male danaines have been reported as having been seen hovering over females, with hairpencils fully displayed, wafting the scent downwards with rapid sweeps of the wings, although copulation was not subsequently observed in these particular instances.

There is one species, the queen, *Danaus gilippus berenice*, which has been extensively studied and the complete courtship is known in detail. As seems to be typical of butterflies, and most other animals if it comes to that, the whole affair follows a kind of behavioural chain reaction, with an initial stimulus provoking a specific response which provokes a fur-

During courtship many male butterflies persistently hover close to the female, occasionally dipping down to touch her briefly and presumably douching her in androconial pheromones, the so-called 'love dust'. This male *Phyciodes actinote*, a small nymphalid, spent several minutes in what proved to be a fruitless attempt at seduction, as so frequently seems to be the case. Photographed in tropical Veracruz, Mexico.

Two male small sulfur butterflies, *Eurema lisa*, perched with their forewings swept forward in a fixed salute to a female who continues to feed, oblivious to their attentions. It is probable that pheromones are disseminated from the males' wing surfaces during this strange action. Photographed in tropical Veracruz State, Mexico.

ther stimulus and so on. In the queen, courtship starts with the aerial protrusion and expansion of the male hairpencils in close proximity to the female's head; this aerial hairpencilling will stimulate a receptive female to land. This 'correct' response from the female now provokes a bout of ground hairpencilling by the male, to which the female reacts by closing her wings, thus giving access to her abdomen for copulation to follow. In all cases, hairpencilling was an essential prelude to a successful conclusion. As is so often the case in the natural world, there are exceptions to the rule and in the danaines, as far as olfactory communication is concerned, the black sheep of the family is the well-known monarch. In males of this species the pheromone dispersal apparatus is greatly reduced and, instead, the predominant method of sexual interaction is far less sophisticated, involving aerial takedowns in which the males simply hijack females on the wing.

Chemical communication has also been demonstrated in the small sulfur butterfly, *Eurema lisa*, in which male pheromones have proved to be essential in releasing abdominal exposure behaviour in the female. The pheromone is disseminated from androconial patches on the underside of the forewings near their bases. The scent is wafted across the wing surfaces by contact, thus allowing this little butterfly to utilise its whole wing as a purveyor of perfume. In Central America it is not uncommon to see a *Eurema* male perched close beside a female who herself is engrossed in feeding on a flower. He sits with his forewing projecting stiffly at an improbable angle, as if in fixed salute to the obliviously imbibing female.

The actual synthesis of male pheromones has only so far been studied in detail in the danaines and in these the procedure is bizarre and unusual and probably applies to only a limited number of other species among the many butterflies known to exist. The principal constituent in danaine hairpencils has been chemically identified as a pyrrolizinone alkaloid, which has now been dubbed 'danaidone' for simplicity. Along with a cocktail of as many as 32 other compounds, this volatile substance seems to provide essential courtship stimuli in most Danainae. The most surprising factor in all of this is the apparent reliance placed by male danaines on obtaining their most potent courtship pheromone secondhand from a plant source. It had been known for some time that these males are strongly attracted to withered specimens of certain plant species, e.g. *Heliotropum*. The experimental findings that male danaines reared in captivity are relatively unsuccessful in sexual encounters led to the discovery that the pyrrolizidine alkaloids absorbed from these plants are essential precursors in the synthesis of danaidone. These substances are also strongly toxic to vertebrate predators attacking butterflies which have absorbed them and thus they possibly play a defensive as well as a communicative role. It has been speculated that only males containing these alkaloids will be accepted by females, thus simplifying species recognition where this may otherwise be confused by the presence of numerous Batesian mimics. Another theory holds that the females assess a male's 'fitness' by his alkaloid concentration, males which have gone to the trouble to absorb large quantities of these chemicals by persistent feeding being possibly much better protected against vertebrate predators. Such persistence in absorbing alkaloids, if genetically determined, would be an extremely desirable trait to pass on to their offspring, thus presumably making such a male a suitable candidate in the competition for mating.

That the crushed and withered stems of certain plants can prove irresistible to male danaines cannot be disputed. A few years ago in South Africa I drove several times along a bush track which was overhung on both sides by sheets of a white-flowered heliotrope and many of these rather straggly plants were squashed beneath the wheels of my vehicle. A day or two later, along the same track, I had to drive with extreme caution to avoid flattening the flotillas of male *Danaus chrysippus* busily probing at the damaged stems as they dried out under the roasting African sun. In the hot, dry valleys of the Andes in central Peru, with their superb stands of woolly-stemmed cacti, I have watched male *D. gilippus* similarly engaged. Male ithomiines have also been seen indulging in these activities and it seems that dissemination of the resulting pheromones may be instrumental in establishing mating 'leks' consisting of sundry related species belonging to a single Mullerian mimicry ring. Several hundred individuals belonging to 20 or 30 species have been observed in these leks, which usually last for only a few days but on occasions may endure for as long as three months.

While the use of scents is unequivocally established in male butterflies, what about their use by females? The ability of female moths to broadcast sexually attractive odours over great distances has long astounded entomologists, so might not female butterflies do likewise, even if to a less impressive degree? Alas, hard facts on this subject are scanty in the extreme, although there is much circumstantial evidence in favour, derived mainly from numerous observations of male butterflies unerringly locating females perched hidden among vegetation. Virgin silver-washed fritillaries, *Argynnis paphia*, have been seen apparently in active solicitation of an approaching male, using two glandular sacs at the tip of their abdomens in presumed dissemination of a male-attracting pheromone. Experiments have shown that unscented dummies may attract a male but fail to incite courtship behaviour, while freshly dead females are a stronger lure to the males than live females which have been artificially de-scented. It therefore seems fairly safe to assume that scent is widely used by male and female butterflies to distinguish both between sexes and between species and, by males only, to recognise receptive and unreceptive females. Once mating is actually in progress a female's attractiveness to other males in the vicinity may not cease and I have many times witnessed mating pairs being disturbed by the obdurate efforts of newly arrived males to grab a piece of the action for themselves. In many of these instances the copulating couple was in an extremely inconspicuous situation and in one case they were completely concealed from view beneath the dense, spreading flower-heads of a shrub. Their apparent immunity from detection did not prevent a second

Danaus chrysippus, the plain tiger or African queen, family Nymphalidae: Danainae. Many male danaines derive their sexual pheromones at second-hand from withered plants containing pyrrolizidine alkaloids which are essential precursors in the synthesis of danaidone. These males are clustered on *Heliotropum* plants crushed a few days previously beneath the wheels of my car. Photographed in savannah in the Timbavati Wildlife Reserve, Transvaal, South Africa.

male from bursting in on the scene and thrusting his unwelcome attentions on the pair. Tenacity was undoubtedly this male's greatest asset, for, not to be frustrated in his efforts, he inserted himself closely beside the male-in-residence and attempted to engage with the already coupled genitalia of the female.

Female pupae may also be remarkably attractive to males and I have seen dense clusters of male *Heliconius charitonia* packed onto a female pupa which was about to eclose, ready to mate with her as soon as she emerged; males will even attempt to mate with pupae, even those of a different species, with frequently fatal results. Both visual and olfactory clues are probably involved in locating these pupae, but in the lycaenid *Jalmenus evagoras* the dissemination of volatile pheromones seems to be the sole attraction, for males are strongly drawn to a female pupa which has been broken open by hand.

Having now considered all of the evidence both for or against mate selection by female butterflies, it inevitably appears that, for the time being at least, the verdict is going to go against selection on the grounds of 'pretty' colours and for selection partly on ultra-violet reflection and much more on scent. If females do basically ignore the colours of their males, then what other explanation is there for male ostentation? One alternative hypothesis postulates that bright colours serve as a means of recognition or a basis for competition between males. In sexually dimorphic species it has been found that the colour of the male may act as a deterrent to the approach of other courting males. Thus, if the white ultra-violet reflecting sections from the wings of a male *Hypolimnas misippus* are added to a previously attractive female's wings, she immediately loses her appeal.

Mating male *Colias eurytheme* expose their hind wings when another male comes near, the sudden flash of ultra-violet light presumably acting to deter further investigation. This is of benefit to both signaller and receiver, for the former remains undisturbed while mating, while the latter will not waste valuable time in attempted courtship of an already taken female. By the same token, patrolling butterflies will waste less time in sterile male-male encounters if recognition of one another's identity and sex can be carried out rapidly at a distance. Territory-holding species, on the other hand, may actually use colour as part of their area-defence system. Physical contact between male butterflies has

Actinote pellenia trinitatis, Family Nymphalidae: Acraeinae.   Even when in copula female butterflies do not lose their attractiveness to other males in the area. This pair, mating inconspicuously beneath the broad umbels of their *Eupatorium* food plant, were approached by a second male who proceeded to insert his abdomen close alongside the female's body in an attempt to couple with her genitalia, even though these were already fully engaged with the genitalia of the first male. This perhaps indicates the active secretion of a female sexual attractant. Photographed on a broad path or 'trace' in Trinidad's Northern Range, bordered by tropical forest and plantations.

frequently been observed and certain tough species of *Charaxes* may have their wings modified as weapons. However, actual physical combat, with its attendant risk of injury to either party, is best avoided and if combat by colour can do an equally effective job in establishing dominance, then it makes sense to use it and to bring its techniques to an advanced state of refinement.

Inevitably there are many drawbacks to these newer ideas, which contain enough theoretical flaws to make more investigation into those puzzling butterfly colours an absolute prerequisite to any clearer understanding of their function.

Egg-laying

By whichever means the two sexes have managed to locate one another, the eventual outcome is a batch of fertilised eggs ready for laying on some suitable host plant. This is an act which I have witnessed remarkably seldom, despite spending much of my life searching for such natural events. On the other hand, I have, on countless occasions, watched female butterflies skipping hurriedly from plant to plant, landing briefly to touch a leaf and then rapidly flying on to repeat the process. This peripatetic questing behaviour by female butterflies is a very common sight, especially in tropical rain forests, and it brings us neatly to an important question. How do gravid females locate a suitable host plant and what characteristics must it possess in order for her to choose it in preference to plants of the same or another suitable species in the same neighbourhood?

Sight appears to play an important role for the butterfly in the long-range primary task of distinguishing its own specific host plant from the jumble of other vegetation around it. Female butterflies seem to be programmed with a built-in search image of a specific leaf shape and any encounter with a plant which fits this image will promote closer investigation. As she homes in on her target her interest in the leaf may be heightened by its emission of a characteristic attractive odour but this does not seem to obviate the need actually to alight, however briefly, upon the selected leaf in order to perform a definitive tactile, olfactory and gustatory examination. She may test the chemical nature of the leaf with the sensitive receptors on her feet, antennae or the tip of her abdomen. Only if the plant feels, tastes and smells right will she possibly proceed to lay an egg; I say possibly for many other poorly understood factors seem to be involved in her choice, particularly with regard to micro-climatic conditions such as temperature, shade and humidity.

Even when the correct food plant has been located the female may exercise a remarkable degree of discrimination before laying an egg. For example, the Neotropical pierid *Perryhybris pyrrha* utilises as its food plant a tree in the genus *Capparis*, which grows in the shady understory of the tropical rain forest. A prospecting female usually rejects, on average, ten trees of the correct species before finally choosing one. She may then spend up to half an hour apparently grading the leaves for suitability, flying from one to another in a repeated test procedure. Even after narrowing the field down to two or three leaves, the final decision still appears to involve a considerable dilemma before she finally plumps for one and starts to lay her eggs. Such labour-intensive and time-consuming conduct indicates an ability to distinguish minutely the suitability not only of different trees, but even of individual leaves on the host plant. It may be that chemical factors are the prime motivating force, but others, such as some leaves being too tough, some too shaded/sunny, or the presence of other eggs already there may also be contributory.

Surprisingly enough many female butterflies do not invariably choose the host plants which are the most suitable for the successful development of their offspring, 'mistakes' seeming to be frequent. This often takes the form of ovipositing on old or withered plants, plants too small to support larval growth, plants of the wrong species, or plants which are biochemically related to the correct species but are incapable of supporting larvae. Generally, however, the female is adequately served by her ability to distinguish satisfactory food plants from the perplexing mosaic of vegetation around her, using her so-called 'botanical instinct'. This seems to consist primarily of a kind of narrow-band filter enabling her to identify a certain chemical or family of chemicals synthesised by her food plant. The chemo-receptors are sufficiently sensitive to enable butterflies to identify similar or identical complex compounds occurring in plants which botanists had hitherto considered to be totally unrelated, e.g. the citrus and parsley families, both of which produce the same essential oils utilised by the North American black swallowtail, *Papilio polyxenes*, as ovipositing and larval-feeding stimulants.

These essential oils are part of the package of chemical defences which have been evolved during the on-going war of attrition waged for millions of years between plants and their main herbivorous enemies, the insects. Unfortunately, like many others, these plants are now in the topsy-turvy position of suffering a reversal in function of their main deterrents, which now provide the major stimulus for receiving the eggs of their rapacious enemies, butterfly caterpillars. In the normal complex run of affairs, while hardly being advantageous for the plant, this situation probably has few deleterious long-term effects on individual plant populations, for so many other factors are involved. However, in Barbados the monarch butterfly has actually extirpated a species of asclepiad and its resident bug, simply by eating all of the plants. This has not resulted in the expected demise of the butterfly, since it has an alternative host plant.

Because of their economic importance, a great deal of study has been carried out on ovi-positional attractants for the large and small white, *Pieris brassicae* and *P. rapae*. Pungent mustard oils in their mainly brassicaceous food plants have proved to be a powerful stimulus for gravid females to offload their eggs, as well as acting as feeding stimulants for the caterpillars which will devour a variety of unusual substances such as flour, starch or filter paper if these are first soaked in the appropriate oils. Tests on small whites established that the females seek out a plant which has the greenest leaves, preferably one transpiring rapidly, both indicators of a plant in vigorous growth, containing abundant protein and highly succulent, two factors which increase the growth rate and survival of the larvae. It may therefore pay you to leave your cabbages in a state of neglect; they will attract fewer caterpillars.

The British Isles, with its changeable summer weather of extended episodes of glowering clouds and chilling rain, all too seldom interspersed with the briefest of warm spells, places severe constraints on the activity of its native butterflies. Females searching for suitable host plants have to bow to the exigencies imposed upon them by the weather, and this may lead to a less than ideal selection of such plants. Studies on the orange-tip butterfly, for example, show that females regularly utilise food plants on which larval survival is poor. The explanation for this seems to lie in the preferability of leaving at least some larvae to survive on a sub-optimal plant, rather than the female dying with a load of eggs left unlaid because too much of the precariously short time available had been spent searching for the perfect plant. These constraints are probably placed on all Holarctic butterflies, which should therefore ideally have as wide a range of host plants as possible. This may explain why specialisation in food plants tends to increase towards the tropics, where adult life and the time available for searching are greatly extended.

This female *Actinote pellenia trinitatis* butterfly (Nymphalidae: Acraeinae) has been attracted to lay her eggs on her *Eupatorium* host plant by a number of clues, of which the most vital is probably the chemical nature of the leaves. She meticulously cements a large batch of eggs to the underside of a leaf; batch-laying is typical of butterflies having gregarious aposematic larvae, as in this species. Photographed in a broad path or 'trace' bordered by rain forest in Trinidad's Northern Range.

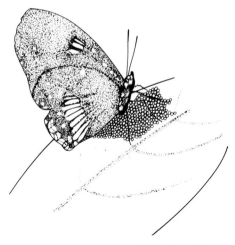

Fig. 6   Female of *Hypolimnas antilope* from the Philippines. She stands guard over her eggs until the dispersal of the larvae which hatch from them.

Although the majority of female butterflies probably offload their eggs directly onto the leaves of plants, a number, such as many fritillaries, have evolved the method of ovipositing onto objects in the close vicinity, leaving their tiny larvae to migrate to the plant later. Many Lycaenidae utilise buds and flowers as hosts, while others use lichens, and at least two species have been seen laying eggs on plant galls. Species whose larvae depend for their survival on ants, such as the Australian lycaenid *Jalmenus evagoras* which lays its eggs on acacia trees, have a singular problem in host location. Before laying their eggs the females feel the leaves with their antennae, presumably to detect any scent left by ants and used by them as 'odour trails'. In addition females may choose to oviposit close to aphids or other colonial homopterans, usually a fair guarantee of the presence, or eventual presence of ants. The *Ogyris* female is able to lay eggs in the midst of ants by 'plugging in' to the ants' own personal communications system, in this case by producing a dispersal pheromone, which enables her to lay without being molested.

While many butterflies lay eggs singly on a suitable food plant, others will invest a considerable amount of time in meticulously cementing a batch of eggs onto a leaf, usually on the underside. Females laying in batches tend to belong to species having gregarious, aposematic caterpillars and large clusters may be the product of more than one female. Certain species lay brightly coloured, nasty-tasting, toxic eggs. Batches of eggs assume a number of designs differing in complexity; these vary from a single row of eggs placed on a blade of grass, through a complex hexagonal pattern, to a carefully arranged stack up to three or four layers deep. Species, such as *Hamadryas amphinome*, precision-lay their

71

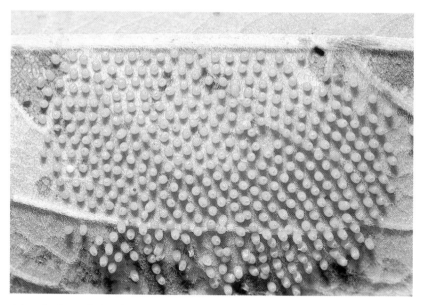

A batch of eggs belonging to *Actinote pellenia trinitatis* deposited on a *Eupatorium* leaf growing in Trinidad's Northern Range. When fresh the eggs are pale whitish-yellow, but soon turn pink. Batch-laying is typical in species with gregarious warningly coloured caterpillars.

The spiky orange larvae of *Actinote pellenia trinitatis*, a nymphalid butterfly belonging to the sub-family Acraeinae, are conspicuous objects as they feed en masse on the leaves of their *Eupatorium* host plant. Such gregarious feeding is typical in distasteful aposematic butterflies such as this species, which is one of the relatively small number within the sub-family to be found outside Africa. Photographed in Trinidad's Northern Range.

eggs in strands which build up into a cluster. Some of these arrangements may endow the eggs in the centre with some measure of protection from parasitic wasps. The female of *Hypolimnas antilope*, however, does not leave such things to chance but affords an extra degree of protection by posting herself as guardian over her eggs. Although leaving the eggs nearest the edge prey to parasites, she is probably able to protect the central core fairly effectively, as has been demonstrated for pentatomid bugs in which female parental care is more widespread.

The co-evolution of butterflies and plants

It has already been mentioned that there is an incessant 'arms race' between plants and insects, which has resulted in extensive adaptive modifications on both sides. I have already referred to the chemical response which has often comprised the main defence employed by a diverse range of plants belonging to many different families. However, the visual nature of a butterfly's host-locating behaviour can also be exploited defensively in various ways and this has been utilised most notably by certain passion flowers (*Passiflora*) in the tropics; they have evolved a bewildering variety of leaf shapes which effectively 'scramble' the butterfly's search image. Armed with a powerful chemical defence and, in some species, the recruitment of mercenaries in the form of ants, a battery of 'decoys' and a minefield of hooked spines capable of disembowelling a caterpillar, these plants would seem to be well placed to win their defensive war against butterflies. Nevertheless, the heliconiine butterflies seem to have evolved successful counter-measures to reduce the effectiveness of all of the *Passiflora's* defence systems, even if they cannot neutralise them all completely.

Heliconiine butterflies are particularly long-lived and this, coupled with a marked learning ability, gives them the time needed to search out their correct food plant, even when it happens to be a 'disguised' species with a variety of leaf shapes. The host plants produce a medley of chemical defences and some species, such as *Passiflora foetida*, can be nauseatingly foul-smelling, a quality for which I can personally vouch. The heliconiines probably utilise some of these factors as host-locating and ovipositional clues, as well as possibly turning them to their own protective use. Some *Passiflora* species have leaves armed with hairs modified to form sickles whose ability to puncture the skin of caterpillars placed upon them has been demonstrated experimentally. Despite this, in some areas the larvae of *Dione moneta* seem to be intimately associated with these plants. Their tiny caterpillars just crawl around in the safe places between the dangerous hairs and then crawl over them, when larger, by the simple expedient of covering their 'bed of nails' with a mattress of silk.

A more 'cunning' and refined form of defence lies in the ability of some *Passiflora* species to produce 'decoys' in the shape of false eggs and larvae. Unlike decoy birds, these are not intended to lure the female heliconiines closer but to dissuade them from further investigation, for

The female of the superb nymphalid *Hamadryas amphinome*, the king cracker, hangs in an inverted position as she meticulously cements strings of creamy-white eggs to her host plant, a trailing vine. Photographed in tropical rain forest in the Parry Lands area of Trinidad.

these butterflies will tend to avoid plants on which eggs or larvae are already present. This reluctance to lay is presumably designed to avoid overcrowding and consequent larval mortality due to factors such as food shortage, increased parasitism and disease. Many heliconiines also have aggressive caterpillars, which refuse to tolerate the presence of others, thus inviting placement of only a single egg per food plant. Passion flowers exploit this avoidance behaviour in a number of ways; *Passiflora cyanea* bears rounded yellow swellings on its stipules, which closely mimic the eggs of its normal antagonist, *Heliconius ethilla; Passiflora punctata* has yellow nectar glands scattered on the leaf surfaces, while *P. gracillima* has scaled the heights of sophistication by bearing numerous tiny, yellow swellings on the tendrils at the growing point. As these fall off after attaining a diameter of a millimetre or so, it strongly suggests that by further growth they would outlive their usefulness as egg mimics. Female heliconiines have been observed to penetrate even this deception by probing with the proboscis and antennae, in addition to tapping with the front legs, to differentiate between genuine and false eggs.

The plants' last line of defence involves the voluntary recruitment of a different kind of insect to act as a kind of platoon of foot soldiers who are always on the alert for intruders. Most passion flower vines secrete a sugary liquid from extra-floral nectaries which are most often placed on the petioles but are also found on the edges, surfaces and tips of the leaves, as well as on bracts and stipules. These are irresistible to numerous species of pugnacious ants which will instantly attack any moving objects, such as a caterpillar, while some will also eat heliconiine eggs. The butterflies probably have no complete answer to these guardians, but contrive to reduce losses by placing eggs on tendrils, especially near the tips. The young larvae of several species, including *Philaethria dido* and *Dryas iulia*, isolate themselves by perching inconspicuously at the tips of small projections, which they deliberately chew out of the leaf margins, for apparently ants do not stray so often into isolated dead-ends, such as tendril tips and projections.

This close interrelationship between the passion flowers and their butterfly enemies would seem to indicate a large degree of co-evolution. However, as in virtually all aspects of butterfly biology, there are contrary views on the subject and in the present state of our knowledge it would be presumptuous to make any definite statements on this matter. Suffice it to say that we have here a rich field for further research.

Chapter 5
Adult Behaviour –
The Daily Round

Apart from time taken by females for egg-laying and by both sexes for courtship and mating, the remainder of the butterfly's day is spent in a variety of ways, including basking, migration and feeding. Lepidopterists from the temperate parts of the world, who lack tropical experience, tend to have a rather restricted view of the food of the average butterfly. They are inclined to see butterflies in general confining themselves to a refined and wholesome diet of nectar from flowers or the occasional sip of the juice from a fruit, the rather disgusting penchant displayed by the purple emperor butterfly, *Apatura iris*, for the liquid oozing from a rotting corpse, not bearing thinking about. On a worldwide basis, however, the less savoury aspects of many butterflies' ideas of a gourmet diet become far more obvious. It takes only a brief encounter with conditions in a tropical rain forest to persuade one that searching along muddy paths, the edges of streams, on dung or even on the malodorous exudate from kitchen sinks will provide a far greater range of species than investigating the relatively few flowers open in such a habitat.

Flowers do, of course, provide an important source of food for many butterflies, both temperate and tropical, and members of the species-rich cosmopolitan daisy family, the Asteraceae, may often be found covered in a variety of different types. The advantage of the multi-floreted head of members of this family is that a large number of individual sips of nectar may be obtained without the energy-wasting need to shuttle from flower to flower. In the British Isles thistles and knapweeds (*Centaurea* spp.) are persistently patronised, while on the sunny edges of forests as far apart as Kenya and Mexico yellow daisies (probably *Bidens* sp.) are constantly haunted by a variety of butterflies from a number of different families. Hemp agrimony (*Eupatorium cannabinum*), with its untidy clusters of pink flowers, usually draws a crowd of late-summer nymphalines in Britain and Europe, while in Trinidad the flowering of the local species of *Eupatorium* is eagerly awaited by lepidopterists, for its small purple flowers present an irresistible banquet to squads of shiver-winged swallowtails and a bewildering variety of other butterflies. This splendid display may be seen at its best in the Parry Lands area of the island, where the construction of broad roadways, hacked out of the rain forest for access to oil-drilling rigs, has led to a proliferation of wild flowers along the broad, sunny verges.

In Britain at least, members of the plant family Lamiaceae tend to be generally avoided by butterflies, since they are better adapted to pollination by bees. A notable exception is the aromatic, lilac-flowered water mint (*Mentha aquatica*) which is readily visited in early autumn by multitudes of small tortoiseshells (*Nymphalis urticae*) and other butterflies. Ivy (*Hedera helix*) also possesses the desirable property of displaying its heavily scented yet dingy flowers in massed heads which doubtless play a significant role in building up the food stores of visiting nymphalines ready for their long winter rest.

One of the most attractive flowers for butterflies in the tropics is *Lantana camara*, a native of Central America, which has been circulated throughout these warmer regions of the world as a garden plant. Unfortunately, it has failed to behave itself and has rapidly become a pest in many countries, with the consequence that biological control methods are now being used to regulate its numbers, with somewhat mixed success. Whatever its drawbacks to man, as a provisioning post for the native tropical butterflies it has arrived as a very welcome addition to the local plant species.

It has previously been mentioned that some heliconiines feed habitually upon the bright red flowers of their caterpillars' passion flower food plant, and this duality of usage of the host plant is not uncommon amongst British butterflies, particularly lycaenids. The green hairstreak, *Callophrys rubi*, and common blue, *Polyommatus icarus*, may often feed upon the flowers of the legumes which support their caterpillars and the orange-tip, *Anthocharis cardamines*, seems especially fond of the flowers of its two main host plants, lady's smock, *Cardamine pratensis*, and garlic mustard, *Alliaria petiolata*. The large white umbels of the typical members of the parsley family (Apiaceae), which are often host to a buzzing crowd of busily feeding flies, bees and beetles, seem by comparison to be of little interest to the long-tongued butterflies, though I recall one notable exception on a visit to Mexico. On the edge of a coffee plantation in the state of Veracruz, a typical member of the parsley family, with very large white umbels, proved to be highly attractive to large numbers of nymphalines, danaines, lycaenids and riodinines.

So far we have considered only the nectar from flowers as a source of food for adult butterflies, since for the majority their life is short and sweet, literally, the nectar acting purely as a source of energy for that short period of intense activity encompassing finding a mate, mating and egg-laying. As a result of the caterpillar's voracious feeding, sufficient quantities of protein are built up in its body to produce first the pupa and then the adult with its relatively large store of spermatophores or eggs. For these nectar-feeding adults, this store of protein is a non-renewable resource and once it is used up then reproduction ceases.

There is, however, a small number of butterflies, belonging to the Neotropical heliconiines (and probably ithomiines) where a way seems to have been found of short-circuiting this vicious circle of protracted larval life followed by a brief adult one. These particular butterflies have taken to using a protein-rich diet, namely pollen, which is freely avail-

Many members of the cosmopolitan daisy family, Asteraceae, are especially favoured by butterflies seeking convenient and rich sources of nectar. The long-tubed florets of thistles are well suited to probing by a butterfly's long slender proboscis, while the habit of crowding large numbers of tiny nectar-rich flowers close together in a composite flower-head saves energy-wasting shuttling from one nectar source to another. This species of *Eupatorium* attracts large numbers of butterflies to its ragged flower-heads in the Parry Lands area of Trinidad. A common visitor is this skipper, *Myscelus amystis*, family Hesperiidae, one of a number of Neotropical species, having striking metallic markings.

able and has been widely exploited by other insects, such as bees and flies, for a very long time. On visiting a flower the heliconiine butterfly rasps its proboscis across the anthers and accumulates a mass of pollen at the base. The insect then regurgitates nectar from the end of the proboscis onto the mass of pollen. Over a period of several hours, the pollen is 'kneaded' with the end of the proboscis, by repeatedly coiling and uncoiling it. Finally the nectar, which is now considerably enriched with protein-building amino acids which have diffused from the pollen grains, is re-imbibed and the used pollen grains discarded. The importance of this complex feeding method to the butterfly is clearly well established, for females deprived of pollen, but given free access to nectar, suffer a noticeable reduction in the number of eggs laid.

This form of nutrition has permitted a radical departure from the normal lifestyle of the 'average' adult butterfly, for whereas nectar-only feeders are, as we have seen, forced to cram the laying of their eggs into a relatively short period of time before they die, adult heliconiines can live to a relatively ripe old age. Life spans of several months are not unusual amongst such individuals and, accordingly, eggs can be portioned out and committed only to the most suitable host plants during this time. It is tempting to speculate on whether the ability to process pollen has been 'forced' upon these butterflies due to their habit of utilising the adaptable and time-consuming passion flowers as host plants (see Chapter 4), or whether the art of pollen-feeding preceded this step and enabled them to transfer from their original host plants to this difficult family where attendant hazards preclude an extended larval life.

The dung of vertebrate animals is a well-known lure for male butterflies, especially in the tropics and, at least in my own experience, more so in Africa than in other continents. Carnivore dung seems to be preferable to the nutritionally inferior droppings so liberally scattered around by the numerous herbivores of the region and it is said that leopard droppings are the least resistible of all. In Kakamega Forest in western Kenya I was fortunate enough to come across a few small scats of predator dung, possibly from one of the smaller cats. It was quite simple to spot this normally inconspicuous material against the dark earth in the gloom below the canopy, for it was completely covered in a living quilt of charaxes and other butterflies. There was constant movement as the avidly supping insects pushed and shoved one another, wings rustling together, to maintain a foothold on the largest and obviously juiciest morsel of dung. Indeed so absorbed were they in their greedy junketing that they would even allow themselves to be stroked gently without being disturbed. This failure to react is so unusual that it is tempting to speculate that some substance in the dung actually acts as a kind of

With their exposed nectaries the flowers of the parsley family, Apiaceae, are not generally favoured by butterflies. An exception is the broad white umbels of this Mexican species which constantly played host to a variety of feeding butterflies, including this attractive nymphalid, *Doxocopa laure*, photographed on the border of a tree-grown coffee plantation in tropical Veracruz State, Mexico.

opiate, dulling the butterfly's ability to perceive danger. (For a list of dung-visiting species see Appendix A.)

In the tropics it is common to see butterflies congregating to 'puddle' on the gravelly margins of rivers, on muddy paths and on the ground where animals have urinated. Close inspection reveals that, as with the visitors to animal dung, these gatherings of puddling butterflies consist exclusively of males. During puddling the actual volume of water passing up the slender proboscis, through the insect and out through the anus is truly staggering, a large droplet of liquid being squirted out of the rear end every few seconds. It is suggested that the butterflies are extracting essential minerals, especially sodium, from the fluid they are drinking, and then the excess water is expelled. Newly emerged adults of both sexes usually have sufficient built-in sodium reserves for normal day-to-day functioning of the body. Many copulating male whites, however, leave behind, inside the female body, a substantial sperm-package which incorporates a high percentage of the male's sodium reserve; this, in turn, is utilised by the female to replace the sodium she has devoted to egg production. The female thus maintains a net sodium balance via the male, while he has to make up his deficiency by absorbing sodium salts

In the tropics it is common to see groups of butterflies gathered on damp ground which has become saturated with certain minerals. These aggregations consist exclusively of males who, by engaging in this 'puddling' activity, are thought to be replenishing vital sodium reserves lost to the female in the spermatophore during mating. This group consists mainly of the pierids *Saletara liberia distanti* (white)and *Appias nero figulina* (gold), with a single *Graphium* kite swallowtail. They are gathered on river gravel in Taman Negara National park, an area of tropical lowland rain forest in Malaysia.

The presence of free water is not apparently necessary in order for a male butterfly to absorb mineral-rich water via the puddling process. Dry stones are also probed, and this nymphalid *Pyrrhogyra edocla maculata* is thought to be daubing the surface with saliva before reimbibing the liquid, now loaded with mineral salts. Photographed on a roadside in tropical rain forest at Tingo Maria, Peru.

from contaminated ground water during the puddling process. The presence of free water is not apparently always necessary, for it is not at all uncommon to see a butterfly probing completely dry and sun-baked stones with its proboscis. In Peru I have watched the lovely red and white nymphaline *Pyrrhogyra edocla* feeding in this way, as well as the heliconine, *Philaethria dido dido*, a particularly attractive jade-green species, and also the semi-transparent danaine, *Ituna iolone phenarete*. In the Smoky Mountains in Tennessee I photographed an admiral, *Limenitis astyanax*, which spent the whole of one afternoon persistently probing a dry dirt road. In these instances, apparently, the surface of the soil or rock is first daubed with saliva, into which the salts dissolve, before it is re-imbibed.

Although natural springs are usually in short supply and favoured puddling spots on riversides are not always easy to locate or reach, the lepidopterist is in the fortunate position of carrying within his or her body a renewable and potent butterfly attractant in the form of urine, a liquid which normally contains a reasonable quantity of the much sought-after sodium. Urine has long been valued as a powerful bait for butterflies, and exotic concoctions consisting of urine mixed with sugar, beer or various aromatic substances, are used by both scientific and

Marpesia berania berania.   This nymphaline was one of numerous species of butterflies puddling on muddy ground behind a hut on the edge of the rain forest near Tingo Maria, Peru (*see* Appendix C). The tailed wings, characteristic of members of this genus, give rise to the popular name of dagger wings.

commercial collectors to secure their specimens. As far as I can recall, Kakamega Forest in Kenya is the only place in the world where I have habitually set forth in the early morning without having gone through the usual ritual of emptying my bladder. Instead, with hurried footsteps I would scuttle urgently along the broad, muddy pathways through the awakening forest to make productive use of the precious liquid by regularly applying it to a particular area. On arrival I would often see a few butterflies in residence, feeding desultorily on the remains of the previous day's offering. The upwardly diffusing aroma of the day's fresh delivery would, however, rapidly exert a magical effect, for in seconds butterflies would begin to drop out of the sky from all directions. Within 20 minutes a couple of square metres of the treated pathway would be transformed into a decorative mosaic of scintillating wings. At this particular location, the first arrival on the scene was usually the delicately tinted green-patch swallowtail, *Papilio phorcas*, closely followed by the huge, wraith-like forms of the mother-of-pearl butterflies, *Salamis parhassus*, which drifted down like tinsel to add a welcome touch of lustre to the sombre forest floor. (For a list of urine-attracted species, see Appendix B.)

I have also found urine very effective in the Far East, but in Malaysia have failed to attract butterflies in anything like the variety so easily lured to it in Kenya. The usual attendants in Malaysia were the three swordtails, *Graphium sarpedon*, *G. doson* and *G. antiphates*, generally accompanied by large numbers of two pierids, the gold *Appias nero* and the white *Saletara liberia*. In South and Central America, however, I have failed dismally to lure a single butterfly to urine, but was assured by a local Peruvian collector that a certain brand of washing powder was extremely efficacious. Apparently there was a riverbank in the area where all of the village women did their laundering and the riverside gravel had become saturated with the washing powder which attracted hordes of drinking butterflies.

The most exciting butterfly feeding ground I ever found in Peru was the very ordinary-looking area of well-trodden earth behind a house on the edge of the rain forest in Tingo Maria. Here the ground was littered with a generous helping of droppings from the scrawny chickens which scratched and pecked around there all day, and was further laced with dog urine and spiced with sweat from the naked bodies of the tiny tots who played and fought on the bare earth. This restricted area of about 20 sq m (24 sq yd) played host to a stupendous variety of magnificently coloured butterflies. Many species would be in regular attendance every day, while just occasionally some gorgeous new creature would appear out of the surrounding forest for a brief visit before returning whence it had come. (For a list of species see Appendix C.)

Even European butterflies seem partial on occasions to the salts con-

Actinote negra sobrina is one of many species of butterflies which can be found puddling on bare ground in the rain forest near Tingo Maria, Peru. It is one of the relatively small band of nymphalids, belonging to the sub-family Acraeine, which is to be found outside their African stronghold, and bears the warning garb typical for the group of orange and brown, probably signifying distasteful properties.

tained in a patch of urine. In the French Pyrenees I well remember a roadside lay-by which was somewhat odiferous as a result of its habitual use as a public convenience by passing motorists. Drinking absorbedly from this somewhat unsavoury ground were small groups of male chalk-hill blues, *Lysandra coridon*, with the odd dark green fritillary, *Mesoacidalia aglaja*. What was so surprising was that these males were able to fly when disturbed, an apparently exceptional feat considering the usually more than adequate consumption of strong red table wines by the average Frenchman.

I have observed a possible case of a butterfly feeding on the frass produced by another lepidopteran on a number of occasions in the Cotswold Hills near my home. Here grows the splendid but locally distributed woolly thistle, *Cirsium eriophorum britannicum*, whose large, spiny, globular flower-heads are often inhabited by moth larvae. Comma butterflies, *Polygonia c-album*, can frequently be seen feeding on the moth larval frass which oozes to the surface via their tunnels, but whether it is the frass or the damaged and bleeding plant tissues which are the attraction is hard to say. I have also seen both commas and speckled woods feeding in much the same way on the seeding heads of the greater burdock, *Arctium lappa*.

Tropical butterflies will often settle briefly and begin to feed on exposed and profusely sweating human skin and a more subtle variation on this theme has been observed in the flambeau butterfly, *Dryas iulia*. In Brazil, this bright orange heliconiine has been seen sipping the liquid in the corner of the eye of a yellow-throated cayman, while in Peru the same butterfly treats turtles in the same cavalier manner.

Ant-butterflies

Ant-butterflies are so named because of their perceived habit of following in the tracks of raiding swarms of the army ant, *Eciton burchelli*, with the specific aim of feeding from the droppings of the ant-birds which are also camp-followers of the ants columns. The ant-birds swoop down on insects which are fleeing for their lives from the relentlessly advancing ant legions and the ant-butterflies follow in their turn to feed upon the droppings of the ant-birds. Why don't the ant-birds simply pick off these butterflies, since they loiter so invitingly close? The answer seems to be that all of the ant-butterflies so far observed belong to the Ithomiinae, a group rich in unpalatable, warningly coloured species which are normally shunned by vertebrate predators, including the ant-birds.

In a major departure from the male-only aggregations associated with puddling, ant-butterfly gatherings are exclusively female. As with the males, this is probably linked to reproduction. For egg production female butterflies need adequate supplies of amino acids and in temperate butterflies, which feed upon relatively protein-rich plant material, these are normally taken in during the larval phase of the life-cycle. However, the vegetation of temperate forests tends to be nutritionally superior to that of tropical forests which often grow on nitrate-deficient soils. It

Comma butterflies, *Polygonia c-album*, have several times been observed to feed on damage caused by moth larvae boring inside the heads of the woolly thistle, *Cirsium eriophorum*, in the Cotswold Hills, England. Whether they are attracted to the larval frass or to sap oozing from damaged plant tissues it is difficult to say. With its scalloped wing margins and overall underside coloration, this species is a superb mimic of a decaying oak leaf. It is one of the few butterflies which overwinters as an adult in Britain.

would appear, therefore, that female ant-butterflies make up this short-age by extracting the small amount of free amino acids present in the droppings of the ant-birds. It is no accident that these butterflies have come to follow the ant swarms which constitute the only predictable source of bird droppings in the forest.

The presence of an ant column is probably betrayed by its characteristic odour which may attract up to a dozen butterflies at any one time, new individuals constantly arriving as others leave. I have never observed ant-butterflies attending an army ant column myself, but have on a number of occasions photographed them feeding on bird droppings in an area of forest recently occupied by the ants. In Trinidad I frequently chanced upon the blue transparent, *Ithomia pellucida*, thus engaged, at times in pairs, or accompanied by *Mechanitis isthmia kayei*, a member of the widespread and oft-mimicked tiger-striped group of ithomiines. In Peru I have photographed *Godyris zavaleta huallaga* feeding in this way, while on one occasion I found *Ithomia salapia aquina*, *Hypothyris euclea* and *Rhodussa cantobrica schunkeae*, individuals from two different colour groups, perched in a neatly arranged trio around a single tiny dropping into which arched each slim proboscis. I have also seen a pierid of the genus *Dismorpha* feeding at a bird dropping, an interesting observation in that this particular butterfly is a presumed Batesian mimic of the tiger-striped ithomiines which habitually accompany ant columns.

Considering its abundance, surprisingly few butterflies utilise fruit juice (rich in sugars and with a modicum of the equally important amino acids) as an adult resource and this is presumably due to their inability to pierce the tough outer skin of most fruits. They are therefore obliged to use fruits which have already been opened up by other insects, such as wasps, or those which have broken open upon falling to the ground. In Britain, speckled wood butterflies are frequent visitors to blackberry, *Rubus fruticosus*, fruits damaged by wasps, and commas and red admirals may occasionally make use of rotting apples. In the tropics fallen fruit is frequently visited by a variety of butterfly species, usually nymphalines, though some types appear to be more attractive than others.

In Kakamega Forest in Kenya I came across numerous small, pinkish fruits scattered along a 5 m (5 yd) stretch of a path. Feeding almost constantly on these were large numbers of nymphalines, notably *Aterica galene*, *Catuna crithea* and *Euphaedra uganda*, the latter a striking purple species.

South American butterflies such as the glass-winged satyrine, *Callitaera polita*, also feed on fruits on the forest floor, which also provide an almost exclusive diet for the huge owl butterflies and morphos which seldom, if ever, visit flowers. Despite the obvious attraction of juicy and over-ripe fruits, in Mexico we observed a range of different types of insect which were strongly attracted to the small, green, unripe fruits of a bush related to the tomato. Although the rind of these fruits was very hard, its stippled surface was eagerly grazed by the jaws of several species of *Polistes* wasps. Also in evidence, and apparently feeding, were numbers of snout butterflies, *Libythea carinenta*, and several species of lycaenid including *Eumaeus debora* and *Calycopis isobeon*. On examination the surface of the fruits proved to be completely unblemished by the attention of the wasps and no honeydew appeared to be present, though the surface did have a slight bloom which may have had something to do with the fruit's undoubtedly powerful attraction.

Also in Mexico, in a highly xeric environment dominated by numerous cacti and other succulent plants, we observed the nymphalid *Asterocampa louisa* greedily supping the copious crimson liquid oozing from a decapitated fruit of a prickly pear cactus (*Opuntia sp.*). The local ants

This *Euphaedra neophron*, one of Africa's loveliest nymphalines, is feeding on a fallen fruit which lies just out of sight beneath the curled dead leaf. Fallen fruits attract many butterflies, particularly this species which is characteristic of the dry tropical forests along Africa's eastern coast from Kenya to South Africa. This particular specimen was in the Sokoke Arabuku Forest, Kenya.

Euphaedra uganda was present in fair numbers on pathways in Kakamega Forest, Kenya, feeding on small pink fruits (which are concealed beneath the outspread wings in this picture) which had fallen to the ground in large quantities beneath a tree. The topwings of this species are of a beautiful purplish-blue, a structural colour owing nothing to actual pigmentation.

In dry scrub in Mexico's Nuevo Leon State, numerous insects were apparently attracted to some substance present on the unblemished surfaces of the green unripe fruits of a small bush belonging to the tomato family, Solanaceae. The most common butterfly was the snout, *Libythea carinenta*, a nymphalid belonging to the sub-family Libytheinae, with only ten members worldwide. In the photograph the butterfly's proboscis can clearly be seen probing the hard surface of the fruit.

seemingly use their sharp jaws to cleave open the ripe fruits and then carry away the seeds to their nests as a source of food, thus giving butterflies access to the juicy pulp in the interior. At the time of our observation, thousands of butterflies were apparently on migration, and the rather tattered specimen we saw feeding may well have been stocking up with extra fuel to continue its arduous journey.

The sap exuding from wounds in trees is another nutrient-rich resource exploited widely in the tropics by beetles, bees and flies as well as by butterflies, including Neotropical species such as the striking zebra butterfly, *Colobura dirce*, and the spectacular blood-red skipper, *Haemactis sanguinalis*. In the Makadara Forest in the Shimba Hills in Kenya, I saw a fallen tree that had been extensively damaged by wood-boring beetles and was liberally discharging a white sap, eagerly supped by several individuals of the green-veined charaxes, *Charaxes candiope*, and the silver-striped charaxes, *C. lasti*, accompanied by a male *Euxanthe wakefieldi*. As with feeders at dung, butterflies drinking sap are remarkably tolerant to close approach by human observers and it is possible that some substance contained in the sap dulls their senses. The frequent strong smell of fermentation emanating from a sap run may give us a clue to the nature of this sedative.

In the North American lycaenid, *Hypaurotis crysalus*, the habit of sap feeding has been developed to a fine art. The larvae attack the Gambell's

In cactus-studded desert near Zimapan in Mexico's Hidalgo State, we noted a rather faded specimen of the nymphalid *Asterocampa louisa* supping the red juice oozing from a decapitated prickly pear, *Opuntia* sp., fruit. Ants may have opened up the fruit to gain access to the seeds, or perhaps a bird had taken a snack of tuna (prickly pear) fruit, but either way the soft pulp thereby exposed had been made accessible to the delicate proboscis of the butterfly. Large numbers of insects, including numerous butterflies, appeared to be on migration at the time and this individual was probably stoking up for its continued journey.

oak, *Quercus gambelli*, and the adults feed on sap oozing from the twigs, utilising this readily available resource in the absence of suitable nectar sources in their xeric habitat.

Basking

Butterflies are recognised as inveterate sun-worshippers and, especially in temperate climes, may spend a significant proportion of each day on a suitable perch, wings outspread, following the sun as it wheels across the sky. One researcher has discovered that English meadow browns spend more time in basking than in all other activities combined. Looking at butterflies as a whole, however, the length of time spent in this inactive state varies greatly according to species, the time of year and the nature of the weather. Species inhabiting the tropics, where a constantly high ambient temperature is maintained throughout the year, spend relatively little time basking, mainly restricting this activity to the early morning or the cool period immediately following a rain storm. Male nymphalids may also pause briefly to bask on a sunlit leaf after a period of puddling or feeding on dung on the cool forest floor.

Butterflies bask in order to enable them to fly, an activity which requires very large amounts of energy; energy which is only available if the flight muscles have reached a temperature of at least 30°C (87°F). Most basking butterflies sit with their wings widely spread, thus presenting the maximum surface area to the sun's rays. Many Lycaenidae, however, bask with their wings closed, leaning over at the optimal angle

Many butterflies, as well as other insects, are strongly attracted to the fermenting sap which runs from wounded tree-trunks. Several sap-runs in Makadara Forest in the Shimba Hills, Kenya were attended by three species of charaxines, including the silver-striped charaxes, *Charaxes lasti*, a species typical of these coastal forests.

In warmer parts of the world butterflies spend little time in basking, a favourite occupation with temperate butterflies. In the tropics basking is often restricted to the early mornings, if then, especially after a rainy night. This orchard butterfly, *Papilio aegeus aegeus*, was basking just after sun-up in sub-tropical rain forest in Eungella National Park, Queensland, Australia. It seems to be in very good condition, and may have hatched only hours previously. In this species the characteristic tails on the tips of the hind wings, found in most papilionids, are vestigial.

to the sun for maximum heat absorption. It is thought that butterflies have exploited the ability of dark pigments to absorb more radiant heat than light pigments in order to accelerate their warming-up process. In many pierids the percentage of dark pigmentation in the wing pattern can vary, seemingly linked to season, altitude and latitude. This idea has conventionally been used to explain the generally greater amount of dark pigment in the wing-bases of these butterflies in the northernmost parts of their range or on mountains where the environment is cooler.

This is explained by the concept of 'reflectance basking' in the whites. This holds that being poor conductors of heat, the wings can only transport to the flight muscles that part of the solar radiation falling on the wing bases. Butterflies with white wings, which are excellent reflectors of heat, have the advantage of being able to use them as mirrors to reflect the rays of the sun directly onto the vital areas of the thorax where they are most needed. This is accomplished by abandoning the normal basking posture, with the wings held flat, and adopting instead a pose which entails holding the wings in a 'V' at an angle of from 10–60 degrees. The black areas near the wing bases, well developed in many pierids from cooler regions, can now efficiently absorb the heat which can be directly transferred to the nearby flight muscles in the top of the thorax. This method of holding the wings enables these whites to achieve far higher efficiencies than other butterflies in utilising the heat from the sun to raise their flight muscle temperature, since it uses the whole of the wing surface with equal effectiveness.

Roosting

After a hard day spent battling with rival males, searching endlessly for a suitable food plant or maybe just basking lazily in the sun, a time comes, towards dusk, when every butterfly must locate a safe spot in which to spend the hours of darkness. Many temperate butterflies are additionally faced with this problem during a high percentage of their daytime lives, for inclement weather enforces inactivity on numerous occasions, especially in the cloudy British Isles. A safe roosting place, therefore, is very important since birds, the main enemies of butterflies, are not affected by such constraints for they are warm-blooded and can search for prey in any weather.

Many butterflies simply secrete themselves inconspicuously at the bases of grasses while others, such as many blues, often adopt the opposite strategy and sit at the very tips of the grass flowerheads. Choosing such an exposed position may seem rather odd until one considers that these grasses are much too long and flexible to support the weight of a bird, which will therefore have to undertake some energetic hovering to reach the butterfly, a difficult and time-consuming exercise. In forests most butterflies tend to roost by hanging beneath a leaf which both protects them from heavy rains and renders them inconspicuous. It is quite amazing how easily a large butterfly, such as the mother of pearl, *Salamis parhassus*, flips neatly upside down into such a roosting place, its pendant wings immediately assuming the appearance of a bleached, dead leaf. Many species roost communally, sometimes returning faithfully to the same spot for many nights in succession. These large roosts occur most typically amongst the unpalatable butterfly groups, which presumably gain mutual protection from reinforcement of the multiple warning patterns seen in such a large gathering, in much the same way as groups of aposematic caterpillars. Establishing such a stable roost quickly advertises the unpalatable qualities of its members to the local predators who consequently learn to avoid them. Some heliconiine roosts have been observed to endure for up to six months, their long-lived members returning regularly throughout their life-spans.

Why other, presumably palatable, butterflies should roost colonially is not, however, clear, since they would appear to be at a disadvantage. The brown and yellow African citrus swallowtail, *Papilio demodocus*, forms roosts of from three to a dozen or more individuals, once again returning faithfully to the same spot on consecutive nights; in Lebanon the Greek mazarine blue, *Cyaniris antiochena*, has been observed at dusk roosting in hundreds. One of my own early experiences with butterflies involved the apparent communal roosting of marbled whites in England. I knew of a small field of long grass where, during the day, this butterfly was common, but, to my surprise, on an evening visit, I searched for 20 minutes or so over a large part of the field without locating a single specimen. Eventually, however, I chanced upon a large number of them concentrated in an area of only 3 or 4 sq m (4–5 sq yd). They were in a spot covered in rank grasses some of whose stems were bent under the weight of the roosting butterflies, a few of which were perched in an heraldic pose with wings spread, soaking up the last few feeble rays of the sinking sun. It seems likely that the whole of the local population of marbled whites was crammed into that one small area, although assembled thus they were highly conspicuous and would presumably suffer heavy losses from any predator fortunate enough to spot them.

In the savannahs of Kenya conical termite mounds are a characteristic sight, their rust-coloured surfaces contrasting strongly with the verdant grasses during the rainy season. Many of these mounds, such as those of *Odontotermes latericius*, are provided with 'chimneys', hollow earthen structures which provide ventilation and cooling for the termite colony. Some of these chimneys contain, in their cool, shady interiors, butterflies which spend the greater part of the day avoiding the heat of the sun by taking refuge in this secure hideaway. The most frequent occupant seems to be the skipper, *Sarangesa lucidella*, often found roosting with its outstretched, clay-coloured wings pressed closely against the smooth internal walls of the chimney. In the tropics butterfly activity is often concentrated into the early mornings when it is cooler, many species roosting during the heat of the day and perhaps emerging for a brief foray before dusk. Lepidopterists in these parts of the world soon learn that the afternoons are best occupied in the same way as the butterflies themselves, that is, taking it easy in some shady spot. The giant Neotropical owl butterflies are especially noted for their crepuscular habits and as they flap lazily and unhurriedly across a forest clearing in the waning daylight, they are easily mistaken for those other creatures of the dusk, the bats.

Hibernation and aestivation

Hibernation as an adult is typical of only a relatively small number of the world's butterfly species, since even in the temperate zones and on high tropical mountains where hibernation is necessary, it is more often undertaken by one of the immature stages of the life-cycle. In the British Isles the hardiest over-wintering butterfly is the comma, which spends the coldest months of the year exposed in full view in the open, protected from its predators by its close resemblance to a dead oak leaf. The other two British nymphaline hibernators, the peacock, *Nymphalis io* and the small tortoiseshell, *N. urticae*, seek more pleasant winter quarters among evergreens, such as ivy, or in hollow trees, often also coming into the comfort and safety of houses and sheds.

Aestivation, the avoidance of hot, dry conditions, is practised by butterflies inhabiting areas with a long and pronounced dry season, when adult nectaring sources and larval food plants tend to be scarce. A

The hours of darkness in tropical rain forests are often characterised by torrential downpours. Most butterflies therefore go to roost, hanging head-downwards beneath a broad forest leaf which acts as an umbrella. The large silvery mother of pearl butterfly, *Salamis parhassus*, is amazingly adept at flipping neatly upwards beneath its living umbrella, where it is surprisingly inconspicuous, resembling a dead bleached leaf. Photographed in Kakamega Forest in western Kenya.

94

The skipper, *Sarangesa lucidella*, can often be found with its clay-coloured wings closely pressed against the inner walls of the chimneys which are constructed by *Odontotermes latericius* termites to provide ventilation for the colony. Photographed in Masai Mara National Park, Kenya.

typical example is the African gaudy commodore, *Precis octavia*, which aestivates for long periods in compact roosts often containing hundreds of individuals.

Chapter 6
A Pattern for Survival

Small creatures such as butterflies have many enemies, and since they lack sharp teeth and claws to defend themselves, they must do so in other, perhaps less obvious ways. As we shall see in Chapter 8, butter-flies have a wide range of enemies whose never-ending selective pressure over millions of years has elicited a diverse spectrum of protective responses, both structural and behavioural. In most instances these involve the use of colour, hence the title of this chapter, but many physical and chemical devices are included in this defensive repertoire. Any collector who has wasted hours in a fruitless search for camouflaged pupae, or who has handled a caterpillar with stinging hairs, with painful consequences, will have experienced at first hand the effectiveness of some of these protective artifices. Their success against the natural enemies of butterflies, such as birds and lizards, is more difficult to assess, but a considerable body of experimental evidence has been pains-takingly amassed concerning the effectiveness of at least some of the plethora of defensive tactics employed by butterflies.

Camouflage in larvae and pupae

In its simplest application camouflage, or in biological parlance crypsis, entails matching the background, examples being a green caterpillar upon a green leaf or a brown pupa upon the trunk of a tree. Not surprisingly for creatures which feed mainly upon leaves, green is a common colour for the caterpillars of both butterflies and moths and those of the European brimstone butterfly, *Gonepteryx rhamni*, and the European orange-tip butterfly, *Anthocharis cardamines*, are typical exam-ples. The larvae of the latter are not only coloured green but also match in shape the developing seed pods of their food plant, and in 20 years of careful searching I have succeeded in finding only a single specimen. Some caterpillars may occur in two completely different colour forms, coincident with the use of two food plants with widely dissimilar leaves. A prime example of this may be found in the African swallowtail, *Papilio demodocus*, which is widespread throughout sub-Saharan Africa. The main host plants are trees of the family Rutaceae, with cultivated citrus trees, such as those of orange and lemon, now being widely favoured.

The fully grown caterpillars are green, broken up by a series of darker areas which resemble leaf blemishes, and thus they merge quite well into a background of citrus leaves. However, in certain localities in South Africa, the caterpillars can be found on plants of the parsley family, Apiaceae. The leaves of these plants are finely divided and fern-like and do not in the least resemble citrus leaves. A high percentage of the caterpillars on Apiaceae are green, as on citrus foliage, but have an intricate series of brown markings which render them inconspicuous in this situation, but would not if they were placed on citrus leaves. Which type of caterpillar will hatch from a particular egg is predetermined genetically, thus posing the so-far unanswered question as to how the egg-laying female determines the correct kind of food plant, assuming that choice is actually involved. The 'correctly marked' caterpillar is, however, normally found on the correct matching food plant and experiments have confirmed that birds are more efficient at picking out the caterpillars on the 'wrong' type of leaves.

Blending into the correct food plant, or even part of that plant, such as the flowers, is not uncommon amongst butterfly caterpillars. The larvae of the pierid *Phoebis sennae* in Trinidad are mustard-coloured with a series of dark rings along the body; this combination helps to break up the uniformity of a uni-coloured, elongated body outline and makes them extremely difficult to spot on their *Cassia* food plant, especially as they usually feed amongst the yellow flowers. On the coastal dunes near Rio de Janeiro in Brazil, certain lycaenid larvae feed on flower petals, their colour varying according to that of the flower on which they are found. This once again poses the major question of how the female of these butterflies manages to lay the right eggs on the right flowers, if indeed she does.

Butterfly pupae are in most instances cryptic and many green pupae are simply attached to the top surface of a leaf blade, exposed both to the gaze of potential predators and to the fickleness of the elements. Some species produce brown or green pupae depending upon the prevailing shades of the vegetation at the time of pupation. The small white butterfly, *Pieris rapae*, for example, produces green pupae on living vegetation while those on dead leaves, walls or on wood are usually brown. Related to this, pupae produced in mid-summer, when plants are at their most luxuriant, are normally green, while late-summer pupae, which must exist through the drabness of winter, are normally brown. Selection of pupal colour is actually under the control of the caterpillar at the time of pupation, since it is able to respond to the general tint of the background. Pupae of the painted lady, *Vanessa cardui*, closely resemble exfoliating flakes of rock, and in desert and mountainous environments, where this species and bare rocks occur together, clusters of pupae may be found in particularly favoured locations. In the Wilderness of Judaea in Israel I have found them hanging in groups under miniature rock overhangs on the walls of a wadi. Their close resemblance to the rock camouflaged them from predators, while the overhanging rock ledges provided essential shade against the burning summer sun and the attendant risk of desiccation.

Just being green may not give sufficient protection when your food plant has large smooth shiny leaves against which any upstanding object will be obvious. The caterpillar of the cocoa mort bleu, *Caligo teucer insulanus*, a brassoline, increases its chances of remaining undetected by orientating itself precisely along the mid-rib of the 2 m (6 ft) long leaf of its host plant, *Heliconia wagneriana*, a close relative of the banana family. Not only does the caterpillar now blend in superbly with the mid-rib, it is also in the lowest part of the leaf where sticks and other objects falling from the canopy will come to rest – extra three-dimensional objects which will render the caterpillar's own three-dimensional body less obvious. Photographed at SIMLA, Trinidad.

Blending in to the food plant is not uncommon among butterfly caterpillars. The dark-ringed mustard-coloured body of this pierid, *Phoebis sennae*, larva makes it hard to spot on its *Cassia* food plant with its clusters of yellow flowers. Photographed in dry, western Trinidad.

Butterfly pupae are overwhelmingly cryptic, often resembling natural objects such as dead shrivelled leaves or broken twigs in an advanced state of decay. Pupae of the painted lady butterfly, *Vanessa cardui*, resemble chips of exfoliating rock and are often placed directly onto a rocky substrate. These pupae were two of many clustered under small rocky overhangs in a wadi in the Israeli desert.

Crypsis in adult butterflies

Cryptic caterpillars generally remain immobile during the day, or at least they instantly freeze when they sense the presence of danger, thus minimising the chances of their being detected. Pupae of course are literally stuck with wherever they happen to be, relying implicitly on their camouflage for protection, for they cannot even attempt to save the day by dropping to the ground, a last-ditch strategy employed by many caterpillars.

Adult butterflies, on the other hand, have to solve the problem of their own innate mobility, which might involve being settled against a number of differently marked and coloured backgrounds during a normal day's activity. A simple, single-coloured livery may not be particularly effective in these varying circumstances and the solution evolved by a variety of butterflies of many families is a kind of 'general purpose' crypsis which, with few exceptions, is restricted to the undersides of the wings. This explains the fact that the majority of butterflies sit with their wings closed or instantly snap them shut in response to a potential threat, thus not only exposing the cryptic undersides, but also leaving the minimum possible area of butterfly in view.

The essential ingredients of this general-purpose crypsis seem to be an abstract mixture of browns, greys and blacks, sometimes giving a vague and ill-defined impression of a dead leaf, but more often serving to blur the general outline of the butterfly, helping it to merge into the typical multi-coloured, multi-textured background of its immediate surroundings.

Certain butterflies, however, do exhibit what are usually considered to be classic examples of so-called 'disruptive coloration', the function of which is to break up the insect's outline whatever the background. Instead of actually seeing a butterfly, a casual observer would see a number of apparently unrelated, coloured and patterned patches, which only close scrutiny would reveal as the familiar wing shape. Unlike the drab colours employed in purely cryptic patterns, disruptive coloration may involve the use of a distinctive and bright design, such as the brown lines on a silver background found in the Neotropical zebra butterfly, *Colobura dirce*. Disruptive coloration is probably most successful in forests where dappled lighting is the norm. The amazingly complex underside tracery seen in many species of *Charaxes* may fit into this category, since they are typically butterflies of forest areas.

Considering that adult butterflies spend a considerable portion of each day at rest on green leaves, the almost total absence of green coloration in their wings is something of a puzzle. The answer may lie in the difficulties involved in manufacturing a green pigment, though where it is employed it can be very successful, as will be obvious from the photograph of the mating pair of green hairstreaks, *Callophrys rubi*. A far more exotic exponent of green as a protective colour is the dazzling Neotropical lycaenid, *Arcas imperialis*, which I encountered for the first time in a Costa Rican rain forest. While walking through knee-high vegetation I was startled by one of these butterflies as it shot out from beneath my feet and danced away like an effervescent blue spark, sputtering in the dimly lit interior of the forest. The spark then flickered and abruptly died as the butterfly went to ground on a leaf some way away. With practice born of long and sometimes bitter experience, I had noted carefully the exact landing-site, or so I thought, for on close examination of the herbage where the butterfly should have been, it was notable by its apparent absence. Thinking that I had somehow missed the spot I stepped forward, only for my heart to miss a beat as the object of my search erupted once more from beneath my feet. This time, however, it landed but a short distance away so that I was able to observe its actions in more detail, what followed proving to be the strangest behaviour I have ever witnessed in a butterfly. Upon alighting, the wings were snapped shut and the brilliant emerald upper wing surfaces were immediately replaced by the undersides which were iridescent green flecked with black. Then, with its feet still firmly in touch with the leaf, it gradually keeled over in a curious slow-motion action, like a kind of emerald 'dying swan' performed to the accompaniment of a thousand serenading cicadas, ending up with its wings lying completely flat against the leaf. During the whole of this ritual it constantly moved the hind wings, one against the other, simultaneously activating a number of black 'tails' at the rear end. These, in fact, resembled antennae; had a predator spotted the butterfly going through its act it might well have struck harmlessly at this 'false head' (more of which later) as it delivered its attack. While not particularly leaf-like in shape, the butterfly's final pose did give it the semblance of a section of leaf which had broken away from the canopy above, only to be caught on another leaf in the understorey below.

Anyone who feels that such an event may occur too infrequently to be worth mimicking should take a walk in a tropical rain forest at night during a bout of heavy rain. The incessant drumming of the raindrops onto the broad, resonant leaves of the rampant vegetation is interspersed at frequent intervals with the muffled thumps of water-sodden epiphytic plants suddenly tumbling to the forest floor. Now and again some ancient forest giant gives up the unequal struggle against gravity, imposed by its rapidly growing burden of water-filled bromeliad rosettes, and crashes to the ground, the roar of its catastrophic surrender reverberating through the forest and sending one ducking involuntarily for cover. The devastating effect on the canopy of this water-mediated attrition is all too evident in the morning, for the ground layer of vegetation is freshly adorned with a living mantle of mosses, lichens, bromeliads, orchids, leaves and all of the other miscellaneous debris precipitated violently from the canopy above. In this environment, the cryptic strategy employed by *Arcas* is therefore very effective.

Ritualised behaviour on alighting is typical of many other butterflies, the European grayling, *Hipparchia semele*, being a prime example. It haunts heathlands and chalk downland, habitats with abundant areas of open ground. The undersides of the wings are very cryptic, consisting of a mixture of greys and browns, with a few white flecks. Prominently displayed near the outer margin of the underside of the forewings are two black spots, each with a white centre, resembling eyes. Upon landing, these spots are briefly displayed, thus presenting an enticing but expendable target for any predator which has zeroed in on the butterfly. A beakful of wing is of no nutritional value to any bird which pecks at the eyespot, causing the minimum of damage to the butterfly, which can then escape. In the absence of any such attack the grayling then proceeds to conceal the eyespots by abruptly withdrawing them behind the camouflaged hindwings. It then turns to position itself towards the sun and tips over onto its side, thus eliminating its own shadow. At this point the grayling virtually disappears, its crypsis being so effective that I have many times been forced to make it reveal its presence by flushing it from the area in which I had seen it land.

Graylings seem to be capable of making an accurate selection of a suitable background and this active choosing is vital for the survival of butterflies, especially those from the temperate areas when cool weather is prohibiting flight. The European dingy skipper, *Erynnis tages*, seems to

The nymphalid *Colobura dirce* sports a livery embodying the classic concept of a disruptive pattern. The series of light and dark areas serves to break up the butterfly's outline to form a confused image at a distance, while close up the dark lines converge persuasively on a false head at the tip of the hind wings, leading the eye away from the butterfly's vulnerable real head. Whether such disruptive colours make this zebra butterfly less vulnerable to predation is open to conjecture. Photographed in a particularly gloomy area of cocoa trees in a disused plantation at SIMLA biological Station, Trinidad. The butterfly is actually feeding on sap oozing from a damaged cocoa tree.

From the considerable proportion of their lives spent perching on green leaves, one would expect far more butterflies to employ green as a cryptic colour. The rarity of this type of coloration among adult butterflies is probably explained by the difficulty of synthesising the necessary pigments. When green is successfully deployed in the cryptic mode it is remarkably effective, as will be obvious from this picture of the European lycaenid *Callophrys rubi*, the green hairstreak, mating on a leaf in the Cotswold Hills in England.

Ritualised behaviour on landing is common in butterflies. The European grayling, *Hipparchia semele*, a satyrine common on areas with abundant bare ground, such as heathlands, has very cryptic underwings which are vaguely leaf-like. Two false eye-spots situated near the outer margin of the undersides of the forewings are briefly displayed after the butterfly alights and then concealed behind the cryptic hindwings. This action diverts a watching predator's attention to the expendable eyespots before the butterfly 'disappears' into its background. Photographed in the UK.

Exceptionally, certain butterflies are cryptically coloured on the upper wing surfaces which are continuously displayed, an example being the guineafowl butterfly, *Hamanumida daedalus*, an African nymphalid photographed in its typical habitat, a savannah in Meru Park, Kenya.

exhibit a highly developed ability to select suitable resting places. Thus of eleven of these butterflies spotted by me as they roosted one evening in an area of grassland, ten were sitting with their speckled brown wings tightly clasping the similarly coloured, dead, fruiting heads of knapweed (*Centaurea sp.*). The eleventh individual was in an equally cryptic pose at the apex of a grass seedhead, its body and wings carefully positioned so as to constitute a natural extension of the plant.

Dingy skippers belong to that special minority of butterflies which dispenses with the normal underwing crypsis and instead sits with the cryptically coloured upper surfaces either partly or fully spread. This attitude is also adopted by the guineafowl butterfly, *Hamanumida daedalus*, a nymphalid which is a characteristic species of the widespread savannah and semi-desert areas of Africa where patches of bare earth are common. It is usually encountered edging its way in fits and starts of flying and walking across the sun-baked earth, its smoky, white-flecked wings fully outspread and blending well with the dun-coloured background. Even better examples of upper wing crypsis are to be found in certain of the cracker butterflies, nymphalids of the genus *Hamadryas* from the Neotropical region. A medley of these, including *Hamadryas februa*, *H. glauconome*, *H. chloe*, *H. feronia* and *H. ferentina*, have the uppersides of the wings cryptically patterned in a mosaic of browns, greys and whites. They perch with their wings open wide, closely pressed against the bark of the tree trunks on which they habitually spend the better part of the day. This group of species tends to be characteristic of tropical dry forest, where bark is often silvery-grey or brown in colour and the butterflies thus blend in effectively, firmly maintaining their cryptic pose until flight becomes necessary. I can vouch for the effectiveness of their camouflage, for the first one usually learns of their presence is when an individual butterfly peels away from its resting place on a tree-trunk, like a wind-blown wafer of flaking bark. Crackers such as *Hamadryas amethusa* and *H. arinome*, on the other hand, sport a beautiful and striking non-cryptic pattern of blue, black or grey markings on the upper sides of their wings. These species also pose with outspread wings on tree-trunks, where they stand out more obviously than their cryptic relatives. However, these two species react differently on the approach of danger, instantly snapping shut their wings in a reaction typical of most butterflies, to reveal a normal cryptic pattern on their undersides.

Mimicry of inanimate objects

An insect which employs camouflage alone for its defence can rely on the effectiveness of its strategy only by remaining on a suitably matching background. Remove the insect to a contrasting one and it is no longer cryptic and can easily be spotted by any potential predator. Mimicry of some kind of inanimate object, which is not sought as prey by enemies, whether it be sticks, leaves both living or dead, or bird droppings, represents an important advance, for it frees the insect, within certain limits, to pose against a range of different backgrounds without losing its protection. Bird droppings or dead leaves occur at random throughout an environment; they do not act with volition in choosing their final resting places and any living creature which mimics these objects can disperse in a similarly random manner.

Mimicry of dead leaves is widespread in caterpillars, pupae and adult butterflies though some are better at it than others. Adults of the European peacock and small tortoiseshell butterflies are vaguely leaf-like on the undersides, but do not stand comparison with the European commas and their American relatives. With their scalloped wing margins, the latter are superb mimics of dead oak leaves, even down to the white, comma-shaped markings on the wing undersides, after which they are named, and which represent a small area of damage with the light shining through. Many tropical butterflies are also passable leaf-mimics, in particular certain swallowtails and nymphalids with 'tailed' wings, where the tail rather resembles a leaf stalk.

Some species have brought the mimicry of dead leaves to a truly astonishing peak of perfection. The most familiar and oft-cited examples are the Malayan dry-leaf butterfly, *Kallima paralekta*, or its African counterpart, *Precis tugela*, as well as many incredible species of the genus *Anaea* from the Neotropical region. All of these species possess realistic 'leaf stalks' on the hind wingtips, while the undersides of the wings are divided by a dark brown line, representing the midrib of the leaf, whose venation is duplicated by the butterfly's wing veins. The combination of shape, colour and pattern can be quite astounding and its authenticity as a leaf can be judged by looking at the photograph of the African species, *Charaxes pleione*. Incidentally, artist's impressions and museum displays invariably tend to figure dry-leaf butterflies posed among desiccated foliage which offers sustenance neither for themselves nor their larvae. Certainly, as far as the Neotropical anaeas are concerned, handy sprigs of faded, dead leaves are in short supply in their more or less evergreen rain forest home. Instead, these dry-leaf mimics often simply sit on living green foliage where they resemble one of the many dead leaves which fall in a continuous, year-round trickle from the canopy onto the vegetation below. They are not unique in this, for numerous kinds of dead-leaf mimicking moths, mantids and bush-crickets also behave in this way. Such mimics are not usually found, as one is often led to expect, among the dead leaves littering the forest floor, probably because of the domination of this habitat by predatory ants, especially army and driver ants, which will devour any living thing across which they stumble. An exception to this is the African evening brown butterfly, *Melanitis leda*, an excellent dead-leaf mimic, which lurks furtively on the shadiest parts of the forest floor.

A number of caterpillars bear a reasonable resemblance to a dead leaf, although, in view of their cylindrical body shape, it is a curled leaf which acts as the model. The supreme exhibitors of this kind of deception are members of the Neotropical nymphaline genera *Anaea* and *Prepona*. My first encounter with one of this group was in the rain forest in Trinidad, when I spotted, by pure chance, a caterpillar of the silver king shoe-

A number of species of the Neotropical cracker butterflies are cryptic on the top surfaces of the wings. They spend most of the day with their outspread wings pressed against the bark of a tree, where they are particularly hard to spot. Cracker butterflies are so named for the staccato cracking sound produced by the males. The species depicted above left is *Hamadryas ferentina*, one of the most abundant nymphalids in the Brazilian cerrado, photographed near Brasilia. Above right: a number of cracker butterflies have brightly coloured sumptuous upper surfaces to their wings. When splayed out on tree bark they are far more conspicuous than their cryptic relatives, and react differently to a potential threat, snapping their wings shut to conceal their gaudy upper surfaces beneath conventionally cryptic undersides. Photographed in tropical dry forest in Santa Rosa National Park, Costa Rica.

A number of butterflies are superb mimics of dead leaves, the Malayan dry-leaf butterfly, *Kallima paralekta*, being particularly famous. Less well known yet nevertheless a fine exponent of the art is the nymphalid *Charaxes pleione*, seen here, below, alongside a number of other nymphalids feeding avidly on predator droppings in Kakamega Forest, Kenya.

maker butterfly, *Prepona antimache*. It was hanging head-downwards from the tip of a leaf, its body extended lengthwise along a silken thread which the caterpillar itself spins as an extension from the midrib of the leaf. In this position it mimics the kind of leaf decay which is commonly found in the tropics, where first the leaf tip turns brown and withers and the necrosis then gradually proceeds up the leaf towards its base. In order to enhance the effect and to provide a natural 'lead in' to its own body, the caterpillar normally excises a few small flakes of leaf and incorporates these brown and crumpled fragments into its silken thread between the rear end of its body and the tip of the leaf proper. Having now formed the appropriate search image for this type of caterpillar I have since found similar individuals on numerous occasions.

Caterpillars of the Neotropical genera *Anaea* and *Prepona* resemble leaf tips which have withered and died. The caterpillar extends the mid-rib of the leaf using a silk strand, and spends the day in an inverted pose where it is notoriously difficult to spot. The incorporation of a few flakes of dead leaf into the silken line between the living tip of the leaf and the start of the caterpillar's rear end gives a natural looking lead-in to the caterpillar's body. This larva (below left) was discovered during the day draped across a twig. At night, however, it returned to its silken line and lengthened it, circling around and around as it added more silk. Strangely enough, though, it again deserted its handiwork at daybreak and draped itself across the twig. Photographed in tropical rain forest in Corcovado National Park, Costa Rica. Below right: few butterflies, even dry-leaf mimics, actually spend much time on the layer of dead leaves on the forest floor, probably because of the hazards posed by marauding ants. An exception is the evening brown butterfly *Melenitis leda*, a satyrine which haunts the gloomier parts of the forest floor. Photographed in Kakamega Forest, Kenya.

To me the most interesting of these has proved to be the larva of a *Prepona* which I discovered during the day in rain forest in Corcovado National Park in Costa Rica. This large caterpillar was probably in its final instar and, in the fashion typical of a fully grown individual, had draped itself across a twig in the manner of a dead, curled leaf which had lodged in that position. Perhaps these larger specimens have outgrown the ability to mimic a withered leaf tip, since they are now longer than the leaves of their food plant. This particular caterpillar had an impressive back-up defence in case of detection. On being lightly touched it immediately hunched its back, bringing into prominence, on either side of its prothorax, two shining purple warts, while at the same time it thrust forwards a pointed protuberance behind the head, which itself bears two short horns. The purple warts now resembled a pair of shining eyes while the two horns, combined with the central pointed protuberance, closely resembled the pointed head and gaping mouth of some of the smaller and highly venomous rain forest snakes. I have found juveniles of the deadly *Bothrops* snake perched in bushes at the same height as this *Prepona* larva, so the deception is certainly relevant. Incidentally, at night this caterpillar would apply itself to the task of extending its silk thread, circling around and around as it added more silk, a seemingly pointless exercise, as it deserted its handiwork during the day.

Many pupae also mimic a crinkled dead leaf, good examples being those of the comma butterflies, in which the surface is adorned with silvery flecks resembling patches of fungal attack. In the African swallowtail, *Papilio dardanus*, the green pupa is keeled and flattened, being placed between two living leaves where it convincingly mimics a third leaf. Many *Papilio* pupae are incredibly faithful mimics of decaying wood, being positioned at an angle to the small branch on which they repose in such a way as to resemble a broken-off twig. The Neotropical *Papilio anchisiades* is even more remarkable since the blunt end of the pupa resembles the shattered, rotting end of a snapped-off twig while the rest of the surface mimics an enveloping growth of pale green lichen and algae.

Mimicry of bird droppings is a widespread strategy practised by beetles, bush-cricket nymphs, spiders and adult moths, but without doubt its most artful exponents are the early instar caterpillars of *Papilio* butterflies. So widespread and successful is this disguise that I closely investigate every suspect bird dropping wherever I happen to be in the world. Since the majority of birds, and thus their droppings, are small, so caterpillars, in order to be convincing mimics, also have to be small. This type of mimicry is therefore restricted to the earlier instars which often change their appearance dramatically as they grow larger. A perfect example of this is the Japanese swallowtail, *Papilio xuthus*, which starts out by resembling a bird dropping and ends up as a snake mimic! A few pupae also mimic bird droppings, in which case they are placed horizontally in a conspicuous position on a leaf.

In general butterfly caterpillars tend to mimic those types of elongated, shiny droppings which have landed intact as a relatively solid lump and more or less retained their structural integrity. There is, however, a different form of bird dropping which is more liquid and, as a result of this, on landing on a leaf it spreads out as an irregular dark patch with the white uric acid paste surrounding it. This is seemingly mimicked by the adults of certain African skippers, such as *Eagris lucetia* and *Netrobalane canopus*, which have the habit of sitting with their chalky-white wings, decorated with irregular black and brown blotches, spread out flat and closely applied to a leaf. This ploy is so convincing that I have been deceived on many occasions.

A final mention should be made of certain pupae which have a luminescent, mirror-like finish, in particular those of certain danaines and ithomiines. They are frequently to be found in rain forests, where water constantly drips from the leaves, many of which are actually supplied with drip-tips to hasten the shedding of their aqueous burden. It is possible, therefore, that in this environment of constantly dripping water, these shiny pupae are droplet mimics, with the added advantage that their slick surface should act as a deterrent to ovipositing female parasitoids.

Decoys and displays

The strategies outlined above are sometimes going to fail since occasionally the randomly probing beak of a foraging bird is going to provoke a crisis. In this event a number of both caterpillars and adult butterflies have evolved devices for limiting the extent of any possible damage and, in some cases, for actually frightening away the predator. If all else has failed and you have been discovered then it is worth while encouraging your enemy to strike at a dispensable part of your anatomy, leaving the rest of you sufficiently intact to make a clean getaway. Experimental evidence indicates that birds, in particular, home in on their prey's head and deal an instantly mortal blow by aiming straight at the eyes. By providing enticing targets in the form of small, false eyespots around the wing-margins, a butterfly can induce a bird to strike at the fragile edges of the wings, from which a small portion simply tears away, allowing the butterfly to escape virtually unharmed. It is surprising just how much of its total wing area a butterfly can afford to lose and still remain a viable flying machine. I have actually seen a specimen of the European wall brown, *Pararge megera*, with around 70 per cent of its wings' surfaces missing and yet it was still capable of actively feeding and flying.

Even strongly asymmetrical wing loadings, caused by the almost total loss of the flying surface on one side, do not necessarily cause undue difficulties, although they may obviously hinder the owner's acrobatic ability in aerial contacts with birds. Partial wing losses are, as a consequence, definitely to be counted as affordable, so the widespread application of eyespots in the highly palatable Satyrinae is not surprising. Capture and release experiments have established beyond doubt that wild birds really do aim a significant percentage of their strikes at

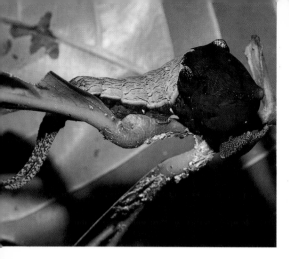

A number of butterfly larvae resemble bird droppings, the most convincing being the early instar larvae of certain papilionids. Above right is the caterpillar of the orchard butterfly, *Papilio aegeus*, on the leaf of a lemon tree in a garden in Brisbane, Australia. Above left, the *prepona* caterpillar, photographed in tropical rain forest in Corcovado National Park, Costa Rica, has an interesting back-up defence if its primary protection of resembling a dead shrivelled leaf is penetrated. Arching its back, it brings into prominence two scintillating blue pustules on its prothorax, closely resembling gleaming eyes and giving the caterpillar the appearance of a small but fierce snake. Below, the wings of many satyrines bear false eye-spots at their hindmost ends, thereby tricking a predator into making an abortive attack on the fragile and expendable wing-tips, leaving the butterfly to go on its way unharmed. Perhaps a bird's beak has been responsible for excising the small section of wing missing from the glasswing satyrine, *Cithaerias pireta*, a typical inhabitant of the gloomier parts of the forest understorey. Photographed in tropical rain forest in the Tambopata Natural Reserve, Peru, one of more than 1,100 species of butterfly present.

False heads, consisting of a dark eye-like patch combined with antennae-like tails at the tips of the hind wings, are seen in many butterflies, although they are commonest in the Lycaenidae. The realistic effect of the false head is considerably enhanced by constant movements of the wings against one another, thereby imbuing the mock antennae with lifelike movements. The function of this deception is to induce predators to strike abortively at the false head, allowing the butterfly to make a clean getaway. This riodinine *Charis chrysus*, the six-tailed brush-foot butterfly, is an impressive example seen here feeding on an ornamental vine in the garden of SIMLA Biological Station, Trinidad.

these eyespots, thus establishing their efficacy under natural conditions.

A somewhat more sophisticated variation on this theme is the incorporation of the eyespots into an actual 'false head', complete with 'antennae' in the form of thread-like extensions of the hind wings. The 'eye' usually takes the form of a black mark against a pale background and the overall deception is considerably enhanced by the manner in which the butterfly continuously rubs its wings up and down against each other, thus producing a lifelike waving of the false antennae. The best examples of this false head mimicry are to be found in the lycaenids but there are also a number of nymphalines and some impressive riodinines which employ the same strategy. The latter group contains the African species *Abisara rogersi* which does an abrupt about turn after alighting, thus perplexingly presenting its false head in the position where its true head should have been, had its landing been noted by a swooping bird. In a number of lycaenids, for example, members of the genus *Arawacus*, and in the zebra butterfly discussed earlier in relation to disruptive coloration, there is actually a series of lines which converge on the false head at the rear end, thus leading the eye of a bird towards it.

Both humans and birds probably find that false-head mimicry is highly perplexing and effective when encountered for the first time, but it rapidly loses it deceptiveness for us, no doubt due to our superior intellect. While in Mexico I came across a group of white, umbelliferous flower-heads, each of which was occupied by five or six feeding lycaenids (possibly an *Arawacus sp.*). I cannot remember any occasion when I have gone so cross-eyed or been so puzzled, albeit briefly, about the nature of what I was observing. My first impression was of seeing several pairs of butterflies *in copula*, in the usual back-to-back position, with the male head facing one way and the female the other. After doing a few double-takes, however, my brain refused to sanction this idea, as the 'pair' was definitely far too short, with too few wings. I had to approach much closer to convince myself that each was really but a single butterfly, at which point the idea of it having two heads hit me. That this could not be true was patently obvious and it was only peering very closely at the butterflies which finally enlightened me as to the nature of their false head mimicry. I must admit, however, that I initially took the 'wrong' end to be the real head, since the constant motion of the false antennae was so convincing, while the real ones remained still.

While small eyespots serve to deflect a bird's beak onto an expendable part of the body, much larger eyespots may be used to try to abort an attack altogether, by actually startling or even frightening off the attacker. Many birds which eat butterflies are themselves small and vulnerable, having many enemies of their own which pose a constant threat, thus requiring constant vigilance. The precipitate appearance of large-eyed owls and other birds of prey can shock smaller birds into instant retreat, so that the sudden exposure of a glowering pair of large 'eyes' by a vulnerable invertebrate might well elicit a similar response. This kind of shock tactic is particularly useful to caterpillars which cannot seek escape in flight, or to large adult butterflies in temperate countries,

Fig. 7   A comparison between an attacking bird's view of a flying owl butterfly and the face of an owl. The large eyes are typical of owls, but notice also how the butterfly's body and head form a convincing beak. Could it be that the mimicking of an owl's face frightens off the butterfly's feathered foes?

where low temperatures may prevent a quick getaway by inhibiting the action of the flight muscles.

The effectiveness of the staring 'face' suddenly displayed by the European peacock butterfly when disturbed has been well established by experiments with captive birds. An inactive peacock folds its wings showing only the black undersides which are vaguely reminiscent of a rotting leaf. If provoked, the butterfly abruptly flicks its wings wide open, exposing four large eyespots, one on each wing. This action is repeated if the disturbance persists, the butterfly meanwhile orientating itself towards the source of the trouble. Captive yellowhammers, *Emberiza citrinella*, omnivorous European birds, were four times as likely to eat peacocks with their eyespots removed than those with the intimidating markings left intact. A jay, *Garrulus glandarius*, which was presented with a peacock, pecked at it enquiringly and then hit the roof of its cage in surprise when the butterfly went into action with its display. However, captive birds rapidly learn that this display represents an empty threat and they eventually eat the butterflies, although this is unlikely to happen in the wild where encounters with cryptic, resting peacocks would be relatively infrequent. Temperate butterflies might occasionally be attacked in the wild while in a torpid state, in which case they would have to rely totally on the degree of fright induced by their display; judging by the experiments described above this may well be sufficient to send their attacker in search of a safer meal.

The African blue pansy butterfly, *Precis orithya*, bears a large, pure blue eyespot towards the hind, central margin of each forewing. While feeding on a flower, the butterfly usually overlaps these spots with the

False heads, consisting of a dark eye-like patch combined with antennae-like tails at the tips of the hind wings, are seen in many butterflies, although they are commonest in the Lycaenidae. The realistic effect of the false head is considerably enhanced by constant movements of the wings against one another, thereby imbuing the mock antennae with lifelike movements. The function of this deception is to induce predators to strike abortively at the false head, allowing the butterfly to make a clean getaway. The tails of this lycaenid *Zeltus amasa maximinianus* are particularly pronounced. It is seen drinking on damp ground in swamp forest north of Kuala Lumpur, Malaysia.

front margins of its hind wings, but counters any threat by suddenly exposing them before flying off. In both the pansy and the peacock the eyespots are probably mainly used to 'buy time', giving them the opportunity to show the startled predator a clean pair of heels before it recovers from its shock.

The use of large, prominent eye-like markings in some tropical butterflies is far more problematical, however, and their precise function is a subject of some dispute. The larger owl butterflies have a single, big eyespot towards the rear of the underside of each hindwing, usually paired with a small spot towards the front margin. There are a number of theories to explain their function, none of which I accept. It has recently been suggested that owl butterflies are excellent examples of the type of display outlined above for the peacock and the pansy. This ignores the fact that only one large 'eye' is visible at any one time on the resting owl butterfly; also, this is permanently visible and so cannot be suddenly flashed to startle a predator.

It is possible that owl butterflies may be mimics of flying owls and the eyespots are used defensively while the butterflies are in flight. These butterflies are noted for their crepuscular habits and therefore any bird chasing one at dusk could also encounter an owl – an encounter which

If the blue pansy senses a threat, the wings are flicked open. However, if the threat is not perceived as being great, the butterfly keeps its eye-like markings covered behind the rear margins of the forewings.

If the danger persists or increases, the blue pansy exposes the two prominent blue marks on the hind wings, usually followed by a quick take-off. Photographed on the edge of Kakamega Forest, Kenya.

could prove lethal. Now, the large eyespots of many owl butterflies, when viewed upside down, are set at the top of two darker, triangular patches, one on each side of the body. The eyes of many owls are also set into two darker, triangular areas, one on either side of the beak. The butterfly should therefore be looked at from upside down, because many birds tackle a flying butterfly by zooming up from below in a frontal attack in order to seize the head, thereby inflicting a mortal blow which will instantly prevent further flight. Thus the bird is highly likely to undertake its final, death-dealing manoeuvre from an angle which will suddenly and unexpectedly present the butterfly in a new guise, with the 'owl face' looking down at the attacker. This abrupt and surprising transformation in the butterfly's status from potential prey to potential predator need only cause momentary indecision, for the potential victim can use those few seconds to make good its escape. The degree of flicker-vision possessed by birds is probably different from our own and the beating of the butterfly's wings may not necessarily destroy the owl-like effect; in fact the bird's own vision may enhance it.

Another very different theory holds that these brassolines mimic *Ameiva* and *Anolis* lizards. Whilst leaving aside the fact that it would seem the height of folly to mimic animals which themselves are subject to considerable predatory pressure, the actual physical aspect of the mimicry seems to me to be highly dubious. It implies that birds possess a quite incredible inability to distinguish between two very dissimilar objects, an idea which is currently fashionable but rather open to question.

Many lepidopterous caterpillars mimic snakes, animals which could be expected to instil fear into a wide variety of small predators such as birds, while the gibbering panic displayed by monkeys on encountering a snake leaves little doubt as to the probable effectiveness of this mimicry against these efficient consumers of invertebrates. The large, fully grown caterpillar of the American spicebrush swallowtail, *Papilio troilus*, possesses two large, yellow false eyes with black centres positioned just behind the head on the prothorax. In common with other snake-mimicking caterpillars, especially those of hawkmoths, these are thrust forward into prominence in response to a potential threat, the larva minimising exposure of its real head by withdrawing it as far as possible below the prothorax. The implication that this is really a snake is reinforced by the way in which the caterpillar thrashes its head from side to side and 'strikes' at its aggressor. Protestations that caterpillars are too small to be effective mimics of snakes fail to take into account that small birds simply cannot afford to take risks with potentially lethal prey; rather they exhibit a pronounced conservatism in sampling any kind of novel food, threatening or otherwise.

Chemical defences

Chemical warfare is not the invention of twentieth-century man; it has been waged on an escalating basis by the insects for eons as just one facet of their defences against predators. The use of defensive chemicals by butterflies in particular is a complex subject, the details of which are only now gradually being elucidated.

Two classes of defensive chemicals are currently recognised as acceptable. Class I chemicals are basically toxic, may or may not taste or smell unpleasant and are able to cause pain, sickness or even death in any predator which consumes them. These are targeted at both vertebrate and invertebrate enemies, although mainly against the former since they are likely to be far less effective against the latter. Class II chemicals are basically innocuous but are designed to elicit rejection on account of bad smell or taste or both. The classification is not always as clear-cut as it may seem, as some butterflies may have Class I chemicals at such low levels that they are effectively innocuous, but because they are unpleasant to taste they may act as a Class II agent. Similarly, chemical mimicry may also be involved, with some butterflies possessing only a Class II chemical which mimics the smell and/or taste of a noxious member of the Class I group. It is probable that many butterflies possess both types.

There tends to be a difference, to both attacker and attacked, in the benefits accruing from the two types of defence. A butterfly with a Class I chemical, which is pecked at and rejected but not killed, obviously benefits by its continued existence. However, in this instance the potential predator is also a beneficiary, for if it had eaten the butterfly then it would have experienced the typical symptoms of violent vomiting and general malaise induced by the noxious chemical in its meal. A bird plunged into this traumatic state by making an unwise choice of prey not only loses its previously hard-won meals but is also incapacitated for up to half an hour. During this time it is incapable of feeding either itself or its young and it is also at an increased risk from its own predators. On the other hand, a bird coming across a butterfly possessing only Class II chemicals need only overcome its initial disgust at the flavour to win for itself a perfectly edible meal, with the butterfly being the only loser.

It is thought that, in most cases, chemical defences are obtained second-hand from the caterpillar's food-plant, one of the numerous and ironic examples of insects successfully diverting a plant's defences to their own benefit. The caterpillar sequesters the relevant chemicals as it feeds, passing them on to the adult via the pupa. As the resulting adult may then pass them on to its eggs, all stages of the life-cycle may be protected in a kind of chemical merry-go-round. It is therefore not surprising that most butterflies known to utilise chemical defences use larval host-plants containing substances which are well known for their toxic properties. Examples are the milkweed family, Asclepiadaceae (Danainae), the potato family, Solanaceae (Ithomiinae), the passion-flower family, Passifloraceae (Heliconiinae and some Acraeinae) and the Dutchman's pipe family, Aristolochiaceae (*Parides, Battus* and *Troides*, Papilionidae).

The best-studied and most thoroughly proven case for the storage of plant poisons for defensive use occurs in the caterpillars of the monarch butterfly, *Danaus plexippus*, and the plain tiger, *D. chrysippus*. Their milk-weed hostplants contain potent poisons called cardenolides which, if ingested in sufficient quantities, can lead to heart-failure and death. However, only half of the lethal dose is required to induce severe emesis, thus ensuring that death rarely, if ever, occurs under natural conditions. An additional complication lies in the fact that many individual monarchs may fail even to pack an emetic punch, as the ability to sequester sufficient amounts of the cardenolides seems to vary from caterpillar to caterpillar. The cardenolide content of the leaves in the various species of the milkweed family, or even within a single species, also varies and in the African plain tiger as many as 80 per cent of a given population of butterflies may effectively be unprotected by their cardenolide content. In North America the western monarchs over-wintering in California feed on a milkweed which is fairly rich in carden-olides and are therefore better protected than the eastern monarchs, of which birds take a heavy toll in their Mexican overwintering sites. The overwintering monarchs suffer in this way partly on account of an insufficient chemical defence derived from cardenolide-poor eastern host-plants (see Chapter 8). Tropical monarchs frequently feed on the cardenolide-rich *Asclepias curassavica*, a widespread weed which is on the increase due to human activities, and presumably these monarchs are the best protected of all. This so-called 'palatability spectrum' in monarchs thus presumes a complex situation where a considerable proportion of a given butterfly population may actually be palatable mimics of an unpalatable minority. It is interesting that some animals seem immune to the effects of toxic butterflies, thereby having overcome the main defences of the species in question.

Considered as food items, members of the Papilionidae, the swallow-tails, seem in general to be among the most acceptable of butterflies to most birds, with only members of the genera *Battus, Troides* and *Parides* appearing to be unpalatable. Their caterpillars feed on members of the Aristolochiaceae from which they probably sequester certain alkaloids and aristolochic acids. When adult individuals of these genera are fed experimentally to birds, they are usually rejected on the basis of taste, with few being swallowed. Caterpillars of the Ithomiinae feed on Sola-naceae, which are well known for their alkaloid content. Tests, again with captive birds, have shown several species to be unpalatable, though not to the same extent as many monarchs. There is currently no positive proof that ithomiines actually sequester alkaloids from their food plants. Certain danaines and ithomiines feed as adults on plants containing pyrrolizidine alkaloids and it is possible that these reinforce the effective-ness of the toxins inherited from the larvae. The situation with regard to the heliconiines and acraeines is even less clear. The caterpillars of heliconiines and some acraeines feed on passion flowers from which it is believed that the adults may eventually obtain poisonous cyanogenic glucosides. These compounds can release highly toxic hydrogen cyanide under certain conditions, giving their possessors a high degree of chem-ical protection.

A common food plant for tropical monarchs, *Danaus plexippus*, is *Asclepias curassavica*, a plant rich in cardenolide content. This individual, photographed on a roadside near Tingo Maria in Peru, had probably fed on this plant as a larva, and would thereby be well protected compared with many North American monarchs which utilise host plants poor in cardenolides. This is subspecies *nigrippus*, noted for the large amount of black in the pattern. It is feeding on *Lantana camara*, a popular nectar source for tropical butterflies.

Butterflies of the African Acraeinae produce copious amounts of a yellowish foam from their thoracic glands when handled and in at least one species, *Acraea encedon*, it is known that hydrogen cyanide is one constituent of this foam. Further research on the heliconiines and their chemical relationship to their food plants is clearly needed, as at least one team of researchers has suggested that these butterflies synthesise their defensive chemicals themselves rather than obtaining them directly from a plant source. Whatever this source might eventually turn out to be, they do seem to be reasonably efficient in repelling attacks by birds and lizards and there is a definite palatability spectrum proceeding from the least protected, more 'primitive' species such as *Agraulis vanillae* and *Dryas iulia* to the highly developed and unpalatable *Heliconius numata, H. melpomene, H. erato* and *H. sara*.

Nymphalines seem in general to be highly palatable to most birds but there are a number of notable exceptions and more will probably turn up as research on them progresses. Most, if not all, North American check-erspot butterflies, *Euphydryas spp.*, in their larval, pupal and adult stages, are unpalatable to blue jays, and recent investigations seem to indicate that certain species of the genera *Hypolimnas* and *Limenitis* may also be less palatable than had hitherto been believed.

Members of the Satyrinae, which have been tested for palatability, seem to be uniformly acceptable, this fitting in well with their generally cryptic coloration and retiring habits. Pierids, on the other hand, exhibit a wide spectrum of palatability, the least edible not surprisingly being the brightly coloured species of the genus *Delias*.

Aposematic coloration

It pays any chemically defended butterfly, in its larval or adult stage, to have a colour pattern as different as possible from its numerically superior, palatable but cryptic neighbours, and for that pattern to be as instantly recognisable as possible. The optimal aim is to enable predators to identify distasteful butterflies at a distance, thus obviating the need to take them into their mouths, for a bird's beak may mangle or cripple a delicate butterfly before its nauseating taste encourages a disgusted rejection. Along with other chemically protected insects, butterflies have evolved brightly coloured patterns as aids to recognition, the so-called aposematic or warning colours. In butterflies they consist either of a single bright colour such as orange or red, or alternatively just one of these along with yellow, white or black in a series of stripes.

Aposematic caterpillars are often gregarious, this reinforcing the visual 'don't touch, I'm nasty' signal and ensuring that the sacrifice of a single member, as a sample in a naïve predator's taste experiment, will lead to rapid protection for the rest of the group. It is surmised that this is not as self-sacrificing as it might at first seem, for all the larvae in the group are genetically similar and therefore saving the life of a sibling by giving your own life is not genetic insanity but an example of so-called 'kin selection'. Aposematic adult butterflies, especially ithomiines and heliconiines, may also form small groups whose members are probably interrelated, and they may often foregather in dense communities over very localised areas of tropical rain forest. In such habitats, this social grouping of both caterpillars and adults may have a further benefit.

Anyone who has sat quietly for any length of time in one of these forests will be struck by its quintessential stillness. This calm is regularly broken by the noisy arrival of a boisterous flock of multi-coloured birds, such as tanagers and foliage gleaners. They perkily inspect twigs for signs of life or throw the assorted, rotting contents of a bromeliad's capacious rosette onto your head, as they search its hidden depths for some tasty morsel. These foraging parties may consist of 50 or 60 birds belonging to a host of different species and each individual keeps its eyes peeled for any notable dietary success by its neighbours; all members of the flock are thus in a position to 'cash in' on any especially rewarding discoveries made by any one of them.

The reverse, however, may also apply, to the possible advantage of aposematic butterflies, for any unpleasant encounters experienced by one member of the flock will probably be noticed and noted by its close neighbours, who themselves will tend to avoid the source of their companion's distress in future. In fact, it may not invariably even need to proceed this far, for it may well be quickly noted that an experienced bird in the flock will consistently ignore a prominently presented food item, such as an aposematic butterfly, thereby possibly inducing a reluctance in all of the birds to sample food with such an easily remembered colour pattern. As a result, far fewer butterflies would need to be sacrificed to the cause of educating the birds in their dietary recommendations, since conditioning one or two birds would effectively condition the whole flock, a factor which may also have important implications in the evolution of mimetic butterflies.

It may surprise some people to learn that aposematic butterflies are not necessarily always garish objects which stand out like flashing neon signs from the surrounding foliage. Indeed it pays any animal to remain undetected as a primary line of defence and, in fact, many warningly coloured individuals, such as the black and yellow ringed larvae of the monarch or the numerous tiger-striped heliconiines and ithomiines, are not especially conspicuous when viewed from a distance of more than a few feet. The object of their colours is not to advertise their presence to every passing predator but to jolt a previously experienced individual's memory when it makes a closer investigation. In some cases, this visual memory prodding may actually be triggered by the sudden display of aposematic colours by a hitherto cryptic butterfly. In Kakamega Forest in Kenya the small nymphaline *Vanessula milca* commonly feeds in groups on damp pathways. The wings are normally closed, exposing the inconspicuous, mottled undersides. The close approach of a possible predator elicits a vigorous bout of wing-waving, which repeatedly exposes the brilliant black and orange uppersides in a strong visual warning. From the fact that this butterfly seldom makes any effort to make any kind of getaway and judging by its generally fearless behaviour and highly aposematic display, I presume that it must be unpalatable.

A rather different kind of unexpectedly sudden visual display, but this time coupled with an active chemical defence mechanism, is exhibited by swallowtail larvae. These caterpillars possess a structure called an osmeterium, a brilliant red or orange forked gland which is normally tucked away in a pouch in the prothorax, just behind the head. When prodded gently, as by a bird's beak, the caterpillar reacts by everting the osmeterium from its pouch. It glistens with an unpleasant secretion of fatty acids, whose odour is plainly discernible even by the relatively insensitive human nose. The function of this strange apparatus has yet to be clearly elucidated, for it seems unlikely to be effective against birds, with their virtually non-existent sense of smell, although douching the body with a chemical mist could adversely affect the caterpillar's flavour and might therefore act as a deterrent. It is possibly more effective against invertebrate predators such as bugs or parasitic wasps. In South America I have found cryptic papilionid larvae crowded together on tree trunks and gently prodding an individual on the edge of the group instantly elicits protrusion of the scarlet osmeterium, not only from the target caterpillar but also from its close neighbours. Disturbance of the whole mass could therefore result in a chemical fog which would presumably form a protective envelope over the whole group.

Although widespread in both adults and larvae, aposematic coloration is remarkably rare in pupae which, in chemically defended species,

Many butterfly caterpillars feed on poisonous plants from which they are thought to sequester various toxic compounds for their own use. This involves the redeployment of the toxins against the larva's vertebrate predators. These larvae are usually brightly coloured, the so-called warning or aposematic coloration being employed as a kind of visual memory-jog, reminding predators with previous distressing experience of the toxic or distasteful properties, that their potential meal would be better left alone. The brilliantly marked caterpillar of the plain tiger, *Danaus chrysippus*, absorbs cardenolides, vertebrate heart-poisons, from its milkweed host plant. In the fashion typical of danaine larvae, it bears slender coloured projections at each end of the body. Photographed in a garden near Mombasa, Kenya.

exhibit a degree of crypsis typical of the pupae of palatable butterflies. This may at first seem surprising until one considers that whereas both adults and larvae can actively secrete noxious chemicals, resulting in their immediate rejection by a predator, no pupa has as yet been found which can actively protect itself in this manner. In the pupa, the defensive chemicals inherited from the caterpillar can only come into contact with an attacker after it has already dealt a terminal blow by rupturing the cuticle. As with everything, however, there are exceptions and aposematic pupae do occur. In Mexico, pupae of the nymphaline *Chlosyne ehrenbergi* are brightly coloured and normally sited conspicuously. In

Swallowtail larvae possess an osmeterium, a brilliant red or orange forked gland which is normally kept in a pouch in the prothorax. When gently poked, the caterpillar instantly everts the osmeterium which secretes an odour thought to be a possible deterrent to the attacks of certain enemies, possibly parasitic wasps. This is the black swallowtail, *Papilio polyxenes*, in Mexico.

Many caterpillars, especially among the Nymphalidae, combine a formidable armament of spines with presumed distasteful properties advertised via aposematic colours. This amazing creature, a *Euthalia* sp., is actually very cryptic from more than a metre, but its formidable defence becomes obvious on closer inspection. The overlapping network of spines forms a defensive stockade, while possibly distasteful properties are advertised at close range by the orange tips of the larva's spiny armour. Photographed in Pasoh Forest Reserve, Malaysia.

Queensland I have seen vivid orange *Delias* pupae perched in full view on the tops of rain forest leaves, as well as accumulations of the black, cream and orange pupae of *Acraea andromacha*, mostly attached to dead stems, sometimes in twos or threes, where they are clearly visible. The occurrence of such a gregarious pupation in an aposematic species is probably another example of kin selection, for the breaking open and tasting of one of the group by a predator should subsequently protect its adjacent brethren. A similar habit is found in the Neotropical lycaenid *Eumaeus minyas* which is highly aposematic and gregarious in all of its stages, the food plants being cycads which contain gastro-intestinal and liver toxins.

Physical defences

Many of the most familiar caterpillars of temperate countries, such as species of *Nymphalis*, are often both gregarious and densely spiny. When disturbed such caterpillars react in unison, suddenly jerking their heads upwards and thrashing them from side to side in a so-called 'aggressive display'. Possibly this is designed to fool their smaller avian predators into believing that this involves a single large organism, which poses a potential threat and should therefore be left alone. However, it could also be that the spines form the main protection and the head-jerking display is merely an automatic continuation of the usual response to the physical presence of parasitic flies and wasps. Some tropical caterpillars positively bristle with an impenetrable thicket of interlocking spines, which probably serve to deter both vertebrate and invertebrate predators, this sometimes being combined with aposematic colours to form a redoubtable and hazardous defence system.

Chapter 7
Variation in Butterflies

Anyone who has visited a butterfly house, examined a pinned museum collection of butterflies, watched a wildlife television programme depicting them in the wild or even had the pleasure of seeing swarms of them in their natural habitat, cannot but have wondered at their enormous variety of colour and form. At first glance an inexperienced observer would probably attribute this great variety to there being many different species present and this is partly true, but a closer examination of any collection of butterflies would show that the situation is much more complicated than at first appears to be the case.

Sexual dimorphism

Whereas in many species of butterflies it is impossible to distinguish males from females at first glance, in many others the males and females appear markedly different. These visible differences between the sexes, which do not relate to the normal differences in structure of the reproductive apparati, constitute the phenomenon of sexual dimorphism. Within the butterflies, the most marked differences between the sexes are in colour and pattern, though there are also examples of obvious structural differences, especially in the shape of the wings. A very good example showing both types of difference within the same species is to be found in the birdwing butterflies, a good example being *Ornithoptera paradisea*. The males are somewhat smaller than the females and are coloured green, black and yellow, while the females are basically dark brown with fawn and white patches. The most obvious structural difference between the two sexes is to be found in the hind wings, those of the male being reduced in area and drawn off to a tail, resembling the more typical swallowtails in the group to which *Ornithoptera* belongs.

The majority of examples of sexual dimorphism, however, are illustrated by differences in wing colour and/or pattern and when it occurs it is often seen that the female is either more cryptic or mimetic than the male who is often brightly coloured. It has been argued that this is a reflection of the greater overall value of the female over the male who, once he has mated, is of no further value, whereas the female must be protected for long enough to lay at least one batch of eggs, thus ensuring biological success both for herself and her mate. Coupled with this has always been the idea that the bright colours of the male were necessary for him to be recognised by the female, although the results of recent research, put forward in Chapter 4, now tend to discredit this idea.

In temperate regions of the world, these differences are best illustrated by some blues of the family Lycaenidae. As their common name implies, the majority of the males of these butterflies are a shade of blue, whereas the females may either lack blue pigment altogether, being instead a shade of brown, or they may be brown with varying amounts of blue. This difference between the sexes is even more apparent in the morphos, many of whose males are a beautiful iridescent blue while the females are plain brown.

A more striking difference between the two sexes is to be found in members of the nymphalid genus *Cymothoe* from Africa, amply illustrated by just two species. In *Cymothoe lurida* the male is predominantly a rich golden colour, with brown edges to the wings, whereas the female is mottled in different shades of brown, with a white band on each fore-wing.

Even more striking is the difference between the sexes of *Cymothoe hobarti*, for here the male is a brilliant red while the female is predominantly white with just a few pale brown markings on the wings. Closely related to these and from the same part of the world is *Precis westermannii*, where the male is black, with an orange patch in the centre of each wing and a metallic blue area on the front border of the hind-wing. The female, on the other hand, is orange, with dusky markings along the wing edges, giving the appearance of many of the acraeas. In a final example, the tiger swallowtail, *Papilio glaucus*, from North America, the species exhibits sexual dimorphism in the eastern and southern part of its range but not in the remainder where both male and female have the familiar tiger-stripe markings. In the south and the east, the female may also be of the familiar tiger-stripe patterning, or it may have a dark morph which mimics an accompanying unpalatable species, the blue swallowtail, *Battus philenor*. The results of some interesting research seem to indicate that the existence of the two female morphs side by side results from a balance between two selective forces, for disruptive colora-tion in the tiger-stripe form and for mimicry of an unpalatable species in the dark form; it is likely that the major force involved in maintaining this balance is predation by birds.

Of no real significance to butterflies in general, but of great interest to collectors, are the rare gynandromorphs, which in various ways may combine characteristics of both sexes. In its simplest manifestation, usually referred to as a sexual mosaic, this may involve what appears to be basically a male or female incorporating in its wing markings some colour which is normally restricted to the opposite sex. In its most bizarre form, gynandromorphy produces a butterfly which is exactly one half male and the other half female, so that at the rear end one side has male and the other female genitalia. Where the sexes are also dimorphic for wing colour, the gynandromorph will have the respective wings on each side marked in the colours of the appropriate sex. It is highly

A number of butterflies are sexually dimorphic and exhibit extreme differences in coloration between the sexes, with the males being the more brilliantly coloured of the two. This is a male nymphalid *Precis westermannii*, photographed in savannah in Masai Mara Park, Kenya. The female is drab brownish orange with black markings.

Seasonal polyphenism occurs in a few butterflies which show striking differences in coloration in morphs produced at different seasons. This phenomenon is particularly well illustrated in the nymphalid *Precis octavia*, whose wet-season form is a particularly resplendent shade of blue; the dry-season form being orange-red in colour. Photographed in Giant's Castle National Park in the Drakensberg Mountains of South Africa, in open grassland.

unlikely that two gynandromorphs could breed, as their genitalia would be unlikely to key into each other. However, as they are extremely rare, the likelihood of finding two to see if they could breed is very remote.

Polymorphism and polyphenism

This is a complex branch of genetics which generates many arguments among the experts but which we will look at here only to the extent that it produces some interesting and unusual butterflies. Polymorphism occurs when two or more forms of the same species exist side by side in the same habitat in numbers which are greater than those which can be maintained by mutation alone. In butterflies, many of the examples of polymorphism are inextricably tied up with mimicry, a subject which will be dealt with in detail later in the chapter. An example of what might be considered straightforward polymorphism, however, is to be found in the European lesser purple emperor, *Apatura ilia*, for in certain parts of its range it can exist in two distinct forms, one with little and one with a normal amount of purple colour.

Some species of butterflies produce very distinct morphs under particular environmental conditions for which the term polyphenism has been coined. This phenomenon seems most often to result from variations in climatic factors relating to seasonal changes. By far the best example is to be found in the African nymphalid *Precis octavia*, which has so-called wet-season and dry-season forms. They differ so much in colour and pattern that when they were first discovered they were described as distinct species, and this is quite understandable when one considers that in the wet-season form the upper wing surfaces are basically red in colour, whereas those of the dry-season form are mainly blue. Along with their visible differences, the two forms tend to have behavioural differences, for the dry-season form is considerably more retiring than the wet-season form, though they do overlap at times, when mixed roosts or aestivating groups may occur. Recent research has indicated that, in this species at least, it is the temperature at which the larva develops that dictates which form of the butterfly will hatch from the pupa, thus those raised at 16°C (60°F) all become the dry-season form and those at 30°C (87°F) will be the wet-season form. This, of course, makes sense, for those raised at the lower, wet-season temperature will become adult in the following dry season and vice versa. The reason for the existence of the two distinct forms seems to relate to differing predatory pressures in the two climatic extremes. During the dry season, the main predators are vertebrates, so a cryptic form of the butterfly is desirable; in the wet season other arthropods are the major predators, and since these do not respond to colour, crypsis is of little use.

P. octavia also possesses polymorphic larvae, with each morph exhibiting polyphenism in its turn. An explanation for this is not yet forthcoming, since a closely related species, *P. archesia*, shows extreme polyphenism in the adult but only ever has one form of larva. Whereas in these African butterflies, polyphenism seems to be a result of differences in developmental temperature, in other species it may well relate to differences in daylength during larval and/or pupal development. Seasonal polyphenism is also well marked in at least one European species, the map butterfly, *Araschnia levana*, which has a spring hatching of adults somewhat resembling a typical fritillary, and a second generation resembling a white admiral, though both generations have similar underside markings. As with the African *Precis* butterflies, temperature seems to influence which of the morphs appears. Some recent research has revealed that in several species of butterflies which do not normally exhibit polyphenism in the wild, maintaining pupae at different temperatures can result in adults with an abnormal distribution of colour pigments.

Speciation in butterflies

Having looked at just a few of the factors which can bring about different forms of the same species of butterfly, it is possible to appreciate some of the problems that arise when taxonomists are attempting to classify them within the order Lepidoptera. The picture becomes further complicated because many butterflies, especially those with a very extensive geographical distribution, show a considerable degree of variation, to the extent that some of them deserve separation into the status of subspecies. At what point one defines a subspecies is somewhat conjectural and best left to the experts, but a few examples may help to illustrate the problems. In the British Isles there occurs a small but viable population of the Eurasian swallowtail butterfly, *Papilio machaon*, which is sufficiently distinct from the individuals on mainland Europe to be designated as a subspecies. Other subspecies are known to occur across the butterfly's whole, vast range, each being maintained by its geographical isolation from neighbouring subspecies. It is this isolation, geographical, seasonal or otherwise, which helps to maintain subspecies, by preventing interbreeding and preserving within each population a slightly different gene pool. With time it may be that they would eventually become species in their own right, as differing pressures could result in the selection of alternative genes within each subspecies. The formation of subspecies is often marked in archipelagos, where a different form may be restricted to each island and interbreeding is prevented by geographical isolation. The classic example of the birdwing butterfly, *Ornithoptera priamus*, which comes from the Australian region, illustrates this well. In three well-marked subspecies the males are either black and green on one group of islands, black and blue on another or black and gold on a third.

Within any single species, especially if it has a wide range, it may be possible to follow a cline, i.e, a progressive change in the overall colour and pattern of individual butterflies proceeding from one extreme of its geographical distribution to the other. In the British Isles, for example, the large heath butterfly, *Coenonympha tullia*, shows a marked change with increasing latitude, such that the English forms are generally darker with pronounced eyespots, but, moving northwards into Scotland, the colour becomes paler and the number of spots diminishes. In a side-by-side comparison between an extreme southern and an extreme northern form, it would appear that two distinct species are involved. A similar pattern of distribution is found in the speckled wood, whose Scandinavian populations are lighter in colour than those found across North Africa. There are many other examples of such clines, and if, in the future, groups within them become isolated, then a movement towards distinct subspecies and possibly eventually species might ensue.

Sundry other variations

There are instances of other rare forms of variation which are of great interest to those collectors who like something unique, but which are of little importance to butterflies as a whole, even though they may put the individual butterfly at a disadvantage. Melanism, an increase in the amount of black pigment, makes an occasional appearance in butterflies and has been recorded in the European and Asian swallowtail, *Papilio machaon*. The opposite phenomenon is albinism, an absence of melanin pigment, which appears to be rare in butterflies, though there are recorded instances of reduced amounts of other pigments. Finally there is homeosis which involves a mix-up during development so that the markings from, say, the fore-wing can become transposed onto the hind-wing; it is hypothesised that such occurrences result from damage incurred during development.

Mimicry

We have already discussed how the various stages of the butterfly life-cycle mimic a variety of inanimate objects, but here we are concerned with the concept of adults mimicking *each other's* colours and patterns. This type of mimicry has always been conveniently divided into two distinct forms but, as we shall see, there is a great deal of overlap between them. Of the two, Batesian mimicry was the first to be described to encompass the notion of a palatable creature, the *mimic*, resembling an unpalatable or unpleasant one, the *model*. From the theoretical point of view, in order for Batesian mimicry to be viable, the number of models should at some time considerably exceed the number of mimics. Since it is aimed solely at vertebrate predators, it depends greatly for its success upon their good memories. In the short term this involves remembering unpleasant experiences from day to day, while in the longer term it is ideal for the butterfly if the predator can store such information from one season to the next. When the mimic has a longer life-span or season than the model, the situation may arise where the mimic may on occasions outnumber the models. The survival of the mimics in this situation is presumably dependent on the ability of predators to remember unpleasant encounters with the models at times of the year when the mimics are absent or rare. We have already considered an example of Batesian mimicry, namely the dark female morph of the palatable North American tiger swallowtail which mimics the unpalatable blue swallowtail. The extent to which the presumed advantage of being a mimic can give rise to dramatic departures, in both wing shape and pattern, from the 'norm' for the particular family, is well illustrated in certain species of *Dismorphia* in the Pieridae. The shape and colour typical of the whites and sulphurs is replaced by the long, slim body and narrow, tapering wings characteristic of their ithomiine models, of which both tiger-striped and transparent groups are mimicked. The effectiveness of Batesian mimicry has been demonstrated with American blue-jays, which rejected on sight palatable viceroy mimics

Fig. 8   These five butterflies from West Africa all belong to the same mimicry ring which is thought to use the two acraeines as models. The species depicted are: (a) female of *Bematistes epaea* (Acraeinae); (b) female of *Acraea jodutta* (Acraeinae); (c) female colour form of *Pseudacraea eurytus* (Nymphalinae); (d) colour form of *Elymnias bammakoo* (Satyrinae); (e) female of *Papilio cynorta* (Papilionidae).

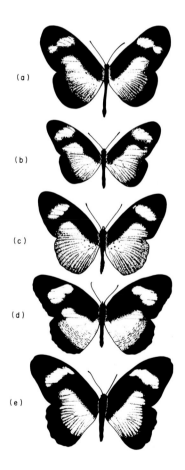

(a)

(b)

(c)

(d)

(e)

presented to the birds after they had suffered unpleasant experiences with the monarch model.

The mimetic concept was later expanded by the realisation that, frequently, unrelated unpalatable butterflies bore similar colour patterns, thus conferring a mutual advantage enjoyed by the whole group. Thus was born the concept of Mullerian mimicry. The advantages are obvious, since a vertebrate predator need only experience the unpleasant nature of a single member of the group in order to avoid all similarly marked butterflies at any future meeting. There is no really simple example serving to illustrate the 'ideal' concept of Mullerian mimicry, which is now seen not to be as straightforward as it at first seemed, partly or perhaps mainly because of complications arising from the palatability spectrum. It would be convenient for mimicry theory if all aposematic butterflies were equally unpleasant, but this is not the case. Even within a well-recognised toxic species, such as the monarch, there is a broad spectrum of palatability ranging from individuals which are inedible to those which can readily be ingested by a vertebrate predator who is not too fussy. These relatively palatable individuals conform to the definition of a Batesian mimic and this phenomenon is now referred to as *automimicry*. It can therefore be seen that within a single environment it is possible to have Batesian mimicry, Mullerian mimicry and automimicry all being exhibited at the same time between and within a range of different species.

An example of this in a natural situation may be encountered in Africa where a system of mimicry exists which, it is suggested, is based upon a central model provided by the very widespread queen or plain tiger butterfly, *Danaus chrysippus*. The model itself has automimicking forms resulting from variation in the amount of toxic cardenolide taken in by the larvae from the food plant, the automimics being visually indistinguishable from their more toxic intraspecific relations. A straight Batesian mimic of the plain tiger is the nymphaline, *Hypolimnas misippus*, although it is only the females that are mimetic, the males being black with a large white spot on each wing. In company with the plain tiger is found its Mullerian mimic, *Acraea encedon*, protected by its ability to produce cyanide, although it has been argued that the plain tiger might be a mimic of the *Acraea*. This picture is further complicated by the existence in Africa of four main morphs of the plain tiger, four main morphs of *Acraea encedon* mimicking the four danaine morphs, and four morphs of the Batesian *Hypolimnas misippus* doing the same thing. Add to this a number of other species of butterflies and various moths, a mixture of both Batesian and Mullerian mimics, and the true complexity of what is known as a 'mimicry ring' becomes apparent. The inclusion of moths in these mimicry rings is not uncommon and in the illustration cited above, the geometrid, *Aletis erici*, is a presumed Mullerian mimic of the most widespread form of the plain tiger, the subspecies *Danaus chrysippus chrysippus*.

South America is notably rich in examples of mimicry rings and indeed it was here that their existence was first realised by the Englishman Henry Bates, who gave his name to Batesian mimicry. In the rain forest areas of the Neotropical region, five distinct mimicry rings have been described, based upon the main wing colour of the participants. These are:

1   The tiger-stripe complex, as the name implies, contains butterflies which are striped in yellow, orange, black and brown. It contains ithomiines, heliconiines and danaines which are accepted Mullerian mimics and also butterflies from other families and sub-families, e.g. Pieridae and Nymphalinae as well as various moths, the status of which is not precisely known.

2   The red complex is centred upon two basically black and red heliconiine species, *Heliconius erato* and *Heliconius melpomene*. What is so interesting about these Mullerian mimics is the occurrence of distinct geographical races across much of South America. Thus, in any particular area, each species has a very similar pattern and coloration, which in turn is fairly distinct from that found on neighbouring races of the two species. In common with the first complex, moths may also be included in this mimicry ring.

3   The orange complex, consisting of orange heliconiines.

4   The transparent complex consists of butterflies with mainly transparent wings, mostly ithomiines, but it also includes representatives from the Pieridae and Danainae as well as certain moths.

5   Although referred to as blue, the final complex contains butterflies which are black, with a blue iridescence on the leading edge of the forewings and yellow markings. The Mullerian mimics within the complex are heliconiines, but also included are representatives from the Papilionidae and other Nymphalidae, which may or may not be Batesian mimics.

The reason for the conjecture about the status of some of the members of the rings, i.e. as to whether or not they are Batesian mimics, arises from the minimal research so far conducted. Recent investigations are beginning to show up a greater degree of unpalatability, at least to some predators, in groups which were previously thought to be quite palatable.

All of the mimicry rings outlined above may be found together in the same habitat, from which arises the inevitable question; why do so many different colour patterns exist when one will do? After all, if only a single warning livery is flaunted by all of the butterflies within the area, then fewer individuals need to be sacrificed in the cause of predator education. Various theories have been put forward to attempt an explanation for this apparent anomaly. One idea proposes that the different complexes have evolved separately in isolation and as climatic and other environmental conditions have changed they have subsequently spread across the whole of the Neotropical area. Each complex is now represented in all areas, with none being at such a disadvantage that it has been eliminated by selective pressure. A second idea, backed up by some experimental evidence and a little personal experience, holds that the

Pictured here are six members of a tiger-striped mimicry ring from tropical semi-deciduous forest at Fazenda Montes Claros in Brazil, in Minas Geraes State. The ithomiines *Mechanitis polymnia* (opp. above right) and *M. lysimnia* (above left) are very abundant Mullerian mimics of one another, and probably act as the central models for the rest of the complex. *Melinaea egina* (opp. below right) is a larger and much scarcer ithomiine mimic, also Mullerian, as is the danaine *Lycorea cleobaea cleobaea* (opp. above left), which is also scarce. A Batesian mimic which seems to be constantly present in small numbers among the others is the pierid *Dismorphia amphione* (above right), while the arctiid moth *Dysschema irene* (opp. below left) is another Mullerian mimic which is present in very small numbers. At other times of the year several more members of the complex are on the wing, including two species of heliconiines. The butterflies illustrated were present in dense aggregations in shaded gulleys in the forest at the end of the dry season.

complexes exist on the basis of a vertical stratification within the rain forest, i.e. each complex flies at a particular height above the ground so that contact with the other complexes is minimal. This stratification works out roughly as follows: the transparents are to be found from 0–2 m (0–6 ft), the tiger-stripes from 2–7 m (6–25 ft), the red complex from 7–13 m (25–40 ft), the blue complex in the upper canopy and the orange complex flying around the trees protruding above the main canopy. Our own first-hand experience certainly puts the transparents at the lower level and the general absence at this level of the blue complex certainly puts them higher up; but the exception is the tiger-stripe

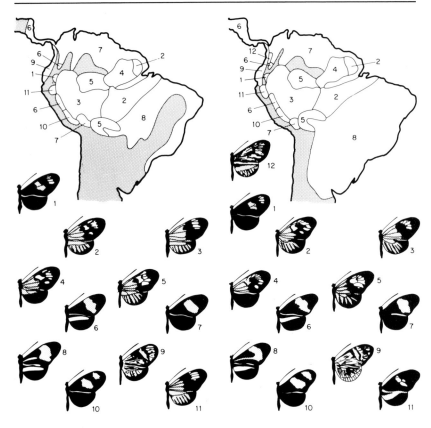

Fig. 9 *Heliconius melpomene* and *H. erato* are Mullerian mimics with a wide distribution across South and part of Central America. They form a number of different races whose variations and ranges are indicated by the numbers. The resemblance between the two different species within the same flight range probably arises from the fragmentation of the rain forest during one of the earth's cold periods. The result of this separation is that they seem to have evolved to match the most advantageous mimicry ring within each 'island' of forest. As the climate became warmer, so they spread out again to occupy their present ranges.

complex, which may be particularly abundant at the lower levels. The reason for this vertical stratification is based upon the amount of light penetrating through the canopy to the various levels below. The crux of the matter is that each different complex should be cryptic or disruptive in colour when in motion at their own particular flight level, but if found by a predator they should have a pattern which is instantly memorable. Certainly, the transparents do appear to coruscate in the gloomy light of the forest floor, making them stand out from the surrounding foliage.

Chapter 8
Enemies of Butterflies

From the viewpoint of their predators the larvae, pupae and adults of butterflies are merely a convenient way of packaging food. Preventing access to this vulnerable resource has involved the butterflies in a major evolutionary contest which is still going on. Any gap in the butterfly's defensive umbrella, whether of a chemical, visual or behavioural nature, is immediately exploited by any enemy which is sufficiently adaptable. This race for defensive or offensive supremacy has no doubt been responsible for the batteries of sophisticated adaptations already detailed in preceding chapters, each fresh weapon in the butterfly's armoury being met by a counter-response in its enemies. We are only now gaining a small insight into this ongoing evolutionary arms race between the butterflies and their varied predators.

Before proceeding it is important to make a firm distinction between the different types of enemies the butterfly will encounter in all stages of its life-cycle. Many invertebrate predators attack mainly the egg and larval stages, whereas vertebrates feed mainly upon larvae, pupae and adults. Unfortunately for the butterflies, a defensive strategy which is effective against vertebrate enemies, such as birds, may be totally ineffective against invertebrate enemies such as parasitic wasps. In fact few protective responses, whatever their nature, seem to be particularly effective against such foes as parasitic wasps and flies, whose own adaptive responses benefit from a similar evolutionary dexterity to that of the butterfly. Many defensive mechanisms are therefore aimed against vertebrate enemies, for here at least there is some chance of staying in front, if only by a short head.

Infectious diseases of butterflies

Butterflies are plagued by a variety of pathogenic organisms, the most important being the viruses which cause 'wilt disease'. Different types of virus are involved and include nuclear polyhedrosis viruses, granulosis viruses and cytoplasmic polyhedrosis viruses. All stages of the life-cycle are attacked though the adults are seldom affected. Larvae in crowded conditions are particularly vulnerable, especially when beset by cold, wet weather. Entomophagous fungi attack a variety of insects including butterflies, the pupal stage being attacked most often.

Arthropod enemies

Butterflies have a spectacular array of other arthropods ranged against them, including spiders, harvestmen, mites, bugs, mantids, bush-crickets or katydids, blood-sucking, predatory and parasitic flies, dragonflies, wasps, parasitic wasps and ants. Protective measures against most of these are difficult to take since many of them are neither repelled nor affected by the distasteful or poisonous properties used so successfully by some groups of butterflies against vertebrate predators. In the same way as the butterflies have evolved the ability to tolerate and subsequently manipulate the defensive toxins of their host plants, so many arthropod predators of butterflies have themselves adapted to the same toxins, even when, in some instances, they have been modified to be even more potent.

Equally, taste does not always seem to be an important or decisive factor in deciding the acceptability of a predatory arthropod's meal, so that the effectiveness of Class II defensive chemicals is largely neutralised. Crypsis and mimicry of inedible objects, such as leaves, are also far less effective, for many arthropod predators and parasites may rely only partly on visual clues to find their prey or host, or even not at all. More often they depend upon their finely developed senses of smell and taste so that while a caterpillar which resembles a leaf will fool a visually adept but olfactorily blind foraging bird, its characteristic odour, no matter how faint, may reveal its presence to a female ichneumonid wasp.

The effectiveness of the prey-locating devices employed by many wasps may be appreciated by some observations I made in Kenya of the large hunting wasp, *Sphex tomentosus*. As it happens, the female does not, in this instance, provision her nest with butterfly larvae but with the paralysed bodies of orthopterans. Every 20 minutes or so this female would return to her burrow, dragging the immobile body of a bush-cricket. These unfortunate victims were all excellent mimics of green leaves, yet this formidable huntress was apparently having little trouble in locating and stinging a monotonous succession of them throughout the day. Had she been a species which preyed upon camouflaged butterfly larvae, then doubtless she would have been equally successful. The possession of eye-spots and other such devices, aimed at vertebrate predators, would probably be equally unsuccessful in deterring such an astute huntress, although one' modification, i.e. bearing spines, may be an effective deterrent to these insects.

Spiders and their allies

It is not really known whether spiders are major predators of butterflies or their larvae. Surprisingly perhaps, adults may not be as vulnerable as small caterpillars which easily fall prey to the juveniles of the fleet-footed wolf spiders, as well as to lynx and crab spiders and their close, non-spider relative, the harvestman. Adult butterflies also occasionally fall victim to hunting spiders, especially to the highly agile jumping spiders

Crab spiders often lurk on flowers and grab any unwary butterfly which arrives. The diminutive females of *Xysticus cristatus* will seemingly take on allcomers, including butterflies much larger than themselves, such as this common European satyrine, the meadow brown *Maniola jurtina*. Photographed in the UK.

A number of crab spiders lie in wait on flowers for the arrival of insects. A female *Misumenops* had been ensconced on this flower which is particularly favoured by *Ithomia pellucida* butterflies, one of which she has captured. Note the fringes on the wings, used to disseminate pheromones. Photographed in gloomy forest in Trinidad.

Butterflies seem to figure surprisingly rarely in the prey to be seen in spiders' webs. The possible reason may lie in the detachable nature of a butterfly's scales which break free, allowing the butterfly to escape from the ensnaring silk. This does not always happen, as is evidenced by this *Anartia fatima* butterfly, a nyphalid which was very abundant in the area, caught in the web of the silver orb weaver, *Argiope argentata*. Photographed in Corcovado National Park, Costa Rica, on horse pasture where the butterfly's weedy host plant was common.

(Salticidae) which can stalk butterflies and pounce upon them from distances of as much as 14 cm (6 in). I have several times seen tropical salticids feeding on lycaenid butterflies, but larger individuals from other groups are probably too much of a handful for these diminutive spiders. The crab spiders (Thomisidae) pose a much greater threat, since many species characteristically lie in ambush on flowers frequented by nectaring butterflies; the colour of these spiders often matches the flower but this is more to protect them from their main enemies, birds, than to avoid their being spotted by approaching insect prey. There is, however, a definite limit to the size of prey acceptable to these spiders since I have occasionally crouched in readiness with my camera in anticipation of photographing a crab spider grabbing an unwary butterfly, only to be disappointed in watching the spider turn tail and retreat beneath the flower. In each case the butterfly was large and powerful and seemingly immune to attack. Again it is smaller butterflies belonging to the lycaenidae and hesperidae which are most often taken by these spiders.

In our experience butterflies do not seem to fall prey to web-building spiders as frequently as one might expect. We have seen butterflies in orb webs but more often we have observed them fluttering briefly against the silk before rapidly extricating themselves and flying off. The answer probably lies in the scales on the wings, which easily become detached, smothering the sticky globules on the silken threads of the web and allowing the butterfly to break free.

In the British Isles we have often encountered butterflies decorated with small, scarlet blobs. These are tiny parasitic mites, which ride around on the adult's body, feeding on the internal fluid by piercing the membranous areas of the cuticle between the segments. In our experience these tiny arachnids seem to occur most often on butterflies (and other insects) frequenting open grassland on chalk and limestone, where their favourite hosts seem to be marbled whites and common blues. It is uncertain whether any long-term harm befalls the butterfly as a result of this parasitism; we have seen a burnet moth, *Zygaena lonicerae*, bearing a broad scarlet sash composed of over 40 mites, yet the moth seemed to be behaving perfectly normally.

Predatory insects

Within this group the true bugs or Heteroptera could well be major predators of the egg and larval stages of butterflies. Mirid bugs have been recorded as having a devastating effect upon eggs and small larvae and this may also be true of two other bug families, the Lygaeidae and Pentatomidae, some of which may attain very dense populations, especially on trees. Pentatomids (shield or stink bugs) attack all stages of the butterfly life-cycle and are particularly insidious enemies, since I have observed them in various parts of the world making a meal of a variety of warningly coloured insects. It would thus appear that they have the ability to overcome the chemical defences of these insects which no doubt at times include butterflies. At times they may be wasteful feeders, taking prey far larger than they can adequately utilise. In the British Isles, for example, I have seen a large and bristly full-grown painted lady larva (*Vanessa cardui*) draped lifelessly across a leaf, the David which had felled this Goliath being the diminutive nymph of a common predatory shield-bug, *Troilus luridus*. I estimated that the caterpillar was at least 50 times as heavy as the bug.

The well-known praying mantis is a visual hunter specialising on moving prey, so only larval and adult butterflies are at risk. The larger mantids, which usually occur in various permutations of green or brown, tend to lurk beneath the flowers where they are less conspicuous to their enemies. They sit in this position peering upwards, poised ready to snatch an unfortunate butterfly with a lightning pincer movement of their wickedly spined front legs. The so-called flower mantids are specially adapted for this ambuscade, for they match the colour of the flower and can therefore obtain a better viewpoint and an instant capture response by sitting openly on the petals. A typical example is a small mantis from Trinidad (*Acontista sp.*) which is decorated with a series of green and white bands so that when posed on white *Bidens* flowers, it is remarkably difficult to spot. It is an impressively efficient

Butterflies are often seen carrying a quantity of small scarlet blobs. These are tiny parasitic mites which ride around on the butterfly's body and feed on its internal fluid by piercing the membranous areas of the cuticle between the segments. Pictured here is a common blue, *Polyommatus icarus*, in England.

killer capable of taking butterflies much larger than itself, such as the beautiful nymphaline, *Anartia amathea*. Such subtle deception is not always necessary, however, for mantids will also stalk butterflies basking on leaves.

Flies as enemies

True flies of the order Diptera constitute a threat to butterflies in three distinct ways. They may suck the blood of both adults and caterpillars; they may spend their larval stages inside the caterpillar, eventually killing it; or they may capture the adults in flight and suck out their body fluids. We will now consider each of these in turn.

Few people, other than specialist entomologists, would expect butterflies to act as hosts to blood-sucking insects. Nevertheless, I have on many occasions seen adults of the tiny biting midges (family Ceratopogonidae) gorging on the blood of both butterfly and moth caterpillars. *Forcipomyia fuliginosa*, which has a confused taxonomy and may indeed prove to be more than a single species, attacks a wide range of larvae over an enormous geographical area. The related *F. aeronautica*, on the other hand, attaches itself to adult butterflies and a *Charaxes numenes* has been seen carrying around 30 of these midges. Morphos also seem to be popular hosts for this species and there are even records of unpalatable ithomiines and heliconiines being attacked.

The bristly-bodied flies of the family Tachinidae are significant enemies of butterflies, restricting their attentions to the larval stages.

The female fly may deposit eggs or larvae directly into or onto the body of the host caterpillar, or, alternatively, she may deposit her eggs on or near the host-plant where the caterpillar will later ingest them along with a mouthful of leaf. Mobile larvae of some fly species will actually seek out a caterpillar and bore into its body through the skin. The fly's larvae develop inside the host, devouring its tissues and eventually killing it. Butterfly species whose caterpillars are gregarious in their early stages seem to be particularly vulnerable and I have several times seen *Pelatachina tibialis* circumspectly laying eggs on groups of newly hatched small tortoiseshell caterpillars.

The third group of flies, the robberflies, which catch their prey in flight, do take butterflies if only rarely. In Africa, for example, a survey was made of the prey of the robberfly *Promachus negligens* from a single locality. The insects recorded as prey were five moths, five ants, an ichneumon wasp, four wasps, two bees, four beetles, one dragonfly, an ant-lion, a termite, two horseflies and miscellaneous other flies, including a smaller robberfly, but not a single butterfly. The probable explanation for this is that the large wings of the butterfly impede the robberfly in its attack, which is normally into the back of the prey's neck.

Wasps

Both social and solitary wasps undoubtedly take a very heavy toll of butterflies, mainly as larvae, but also on occasions as adults. Social wasps are rapacious and highly efficient predators with well-developed

Certain praying mantids are beautifully adapted for lying in ambush on flowers, ready to grab arriving insects in their fiercely hooked pincer-like front legs. This small *Acontista* sp. mantis in Trinidad has managed to kill prey much larger than herself, a coolie butterfly, *Anartia amathea*.

Tiny biting midges, flies of the family Ceratopogonidae, suck the blood of both caterpillars and adult butterflies. This minute *Forcipomyia*, possibly *F. fuliginosa*, is gorging on the spectacular spiny larva of the nymphalid *Historis odius* in tropical dry forest in Santa Rosa National Park, Costa Rica.

hunting instincts and powerful jaws capable of dealing with a wide range of prey. Many wasps stake out a hunting area next to clumps of flowers which are being regularly visited by insects. They pounce upon and decapitate these unfortunate nectar seekers, including butterflies, which may also be taken while on the wing. Social wasps also devote a large part of each day to a painstaking search of the vegetation, plucking off caterpillars and rapidly transforming them from a highly organised living organism into a neatly rolled package of pulped convenience food for their hungry larvae. The nests of social wasps may attain a considerable size and contain innumerable hungry mouths and consequently the local population of soft-bodied invertebrates, including butterfly larvae, may rapidly be decimated. These nests may also occur at remarkable densities; for example, I have found scores of nests of *Polistes* species placed 2 or 3 m (2 or 3 yd) apart in an area of dry scrub north of Santiago in Chile; in Mexico, nests of several related species liberally littered areas of dry acacia woodland near Ciudad Victoria. It seems possible, therefore, that the toll of butterfly caterpillars taken by these wasps has been underestimated and that they are, in reality, major enemies of butterflies. Whereas social wasps are opportunistic predators which include butterflies among a multitude of other prey, certain solitary hunting-wasps prey specifically upon caterpillars, though they probably do not exert much of an effect upon butterfly populations.

Another group of wasps also attacks caterpillars, often restricting their attentions to one or two closely related species or even to a single species.

Eggs are deposited onto or into the caterpillar and the wasp larvae then feed upon the tissues of their host, eventually emerging and pupating beside its now moribund body. Animals exhibiting this form of behaviour, which eventually results in the death of the host, are referred to as parasitoids, for this really represents a specialised form of predation rather than the simple parasitism displayed by fleas and other bloodsuckers, which exploit their hosts without killing them.

As we have already seen, many butterfly caterpillars display a formidable defensive panoply of dense hairs and spines which is probably an effective way of deterring both parasitoid and vertebrate enemies. It is likely, however, that many parasitic wasps circumvent this defence by always laying their eggs on tiny, newly hatched caterpillars, which are far more vulnerable, not yet having developed their protective embellishments of hairs and spines. There are even wasps so tiny that they can lay their own eggs inside the eggs of butterflies, the wasp larvae successfully exploiting the tiny reserves of food therein for their own development.

Perhaps the most thoroughly studied of these parasitoids is the tiny braconid wasp, *Apanteles glomeratus*, which in Europe commonly exploits larvae of various whites of the genus *Pieris*. I have watched the diminutive females of this wasp ovipositing on newly hatched larvae of the cabbage white, *Pieris brassicae*, and the usual sequence of events is as follows. Hatching of the butterfly eggs and the emergence of the female wasps from their cocoons appears to be synchronous, or nearly so, since it is only in the newly emerged larvae that the wasp can lay her eggs. To

Some of the deadliest enemies confronting butterflies in their larval stages are the bristly bodied flies of the family Tachinidae. Female tachinids deposit eggs or larvae directly onto the caterpillars or nearby where they are likely to be ingested along with a mouthful of food plant. The fly larvae develop inside the caterpillar, eventually killing it. This female *Pelatachina tibialis* is paying close attention to a nest of newly hatched caterpillars of the common European nymphalid *Nymphalis urticae*, the small tortoiseshell. Photographed in the UK.

Social wasps are highly efficient predators of other insects, and take a very heavy toll of lepidoptera in their larval stages. This *Polybia tinctipennis* wasp in rain forest near Tingo Maria in Peru has just finished transforming a living caterpillar into a neatly bundled protein package of a convenient size for carrying to the nest.

Caterpillars sometimes suffer heavily from the attentions of parasitic wasps, gregarious species being particularly at risk. The female wasp oviposits into the body of the caterpillar and the wasp larvae proceed to devour their host, eventually killing it once they themselves are fully developed. Such a parasitic way of life, whereby the host is eventually killed, is really a specialised form of predation, and the name parasitoid is often used to describe these insects. Pictured is the minute female of the braconid *Apanteles glomeratus* ovipositing on helpless newly hatched larvae of the large white *Pieris brassicae* which suffers heavily from attacks by this wasp. Photographed in the UK.

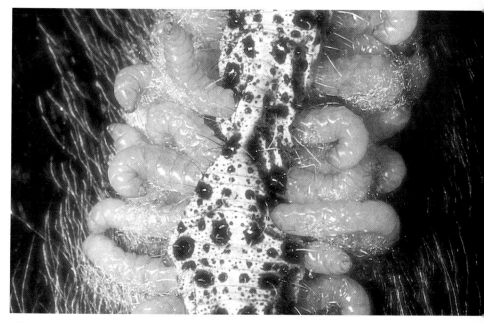

Only when the larvae of the tiny braconid wasp *Apanteles glomeratus* have finished feeding on their mobile host does the full nightmare of what has been happening unseen inside the caterpillar become apparent as a legion of wriggling grubs bore their way out through the caterpillar's rapidly crumpling skin. Photographed in the UK.

do so, she adopts a specialised stance, standing very high on her legs and bending her abdomen forwards to lay each egg. The larvae thrash around in a defensive manner which, despite their tiny size, tends to make her rather jumpy. At first she seems markedly reluctant to set foot on the squirming mass of caterpillars and consequently she initially concentrates on those unfortunates on the periphery. She does, however, execute her egg-laying with considerable application so that eventually the majority of the caterpillars are parasitised. The wasp larvae develop invisibly within the growing caterpillar, taking care not to provoke their host's, and therefore their own, premature death by damaging its vital organs. Finally, the last instar caterpillar is ready to pupate and it is at this point that the horror of what has been happening inside it becomes apparent, as up to 50 glistening, wriggling *Apanteles* grubs bore their way out, *en masse*, through the rapidly collapsing skin of their erstwhile host. They speedily spin cocoons of yellowish silk and it is these, flanking the dead, crumpled remains of cabbage white caterpillars, that are a familiar sight to most people and perhaps something of a puzzle to many. Many parasitoids locate their host by scent and the strong odour of frass produced by aggregations of caterpillars is intensely attractive to searching female wasps. This may therefore explain why many caterpillars, including those of the large white, practise ballistic sanitation, i.e. they raise up their rear ends and catapult their droppings away from the food plant. This has the additional function of avoiding contamination of the food plant by decaying faeces.

Large white caterpillars are also vulnerable as they prepare to pupate, for another minute parasitoid, the chalcid, *Pteromalus puparum*, is waiting for just this moment. Sensing that the time is right, the female wasp seeks out the caterpillar and may actually ride on its back as it seeks a suitable sheltered site in which to pupate. This ensures that the wasp is in attendance at the actual moment of pupation, for she is only capable of piercing the soft skin of a newly formed pupa with her tiny ovipositor.

This habit of laying eggs chiefly in fresh pupae is probably widespread and with good reason, for the mature butterfly pupa is far from defence-less against such enemies; its hard surface is often very polished and slippery, presenting a difficult foothold even when stationary. The presence of a female parasitoid walking over its surface may also provoke violent wriggling movements of the pupa, which can result in the tiny wasp being flung off bodily into the air. Other pupae, such as that of the speckled wood, are capable of only feeble movements and rely on the very tough, slick surface of their cuticle to act as a protective armour.

The successful insertion of an egg inside a host caterpillar is not, however, necessarily the final act in the drama, for the caterpillar may immediately deploy physiological counter-measures against the invaders. The most commonly recorded response is to encapsulate the egg or larva using agglomerations of haematocytes, which are the equivalent of our white blood cells. These surround the intruder in large numbers, though the parasitoid larvae may be able to prevent this by violent wriggling; if this fails they are eventually encapsulated and die. Just how many pro-spective parasitoids are successfully attacked in this way is open to question, but these wasps are well adapted to their hosts and in many instances may overcome any counter-measures instituted by the cater-pillar. It is quite possible, on the other hand, that resistance to encap-sulation may be the reason for the very limited host range selected by many parasitic wasps, only those to which immunity has been developed being utilised without fear of a counter-attack. Parasitoid larvae of the tachinid flies have advanced even further and are often enclosed in a respiratory sheath, which is probably a modification of the host's defence mechanism.

Beetles

Polyphagous beetles probably eat large numbers of butterfly eggs as well as small caterpillars. However, there are instances where a species of both a butterfly and a beetle restrict their diet to a single host plant, and when this happens complications can arise. In Costa Rica *Heliconius hewitsoni* lays its eggs in batches of from seven to thirteen on plants of the passion flower *Passiflora pittieri*, preferring young shoots in the range 18–32 mm. These shoots are often inhabited by numerous orange flea-beetles (Chrysomelidae, Alticinae) of an unidentified species, which also utilise the same food plant. *H. hewitsoni* females show a significant reluctance to deposit eggs on shoots bearing beetles. When beetles invade shoots already occupied by the butterfly's eggs they appear to be highly destructive, sometimes simply eating all the eggs which happen to be in the way, while at other times they bite a slice out of every egg as a prelude to finishing off either the rest of the eggs or the shoot. When beetle competition is intensive, butterfly reproduction may be reduced almost to zero and the host plant itself may be severely depleted locally. The dynamics of this relationship seem to have changed drastically during periods of research spanning only three to four years, implying that tropical systems might not always be quite as stable as we tend to assume.

Vertebrate predators

Frogs, toads, lizards, birds and a variety of mammals have all been recorded as including butterflies in their diets. Of these, by far the most important are the birds, who are almost certainly the main selective agents responsible for the many defensive artifices evolved by butterflies in all stages of their life-cycle. Birds probably prey mainly on largish larvae and the pupae of butterflies but they will also take adults and even eggs. There can be no really secure hiding places for butterflies at any stage of their life-cycle, since the wide-ranging and thorough foraging strategies typical of birds ensure that all available niches are explored.

Birds hunt exclusively by sight and the excellent visual acuity of some of the birds of prey is well known to most people. I have borne witness to their remarkable eyesight and in particular the activities of an Australian kookaburra come to mind. This individual was perched about 3 m (9 ft) off the ground on a eucalyptus branch. Peering intently into the gathering gloom of dusk, it would regularly launch itself into the long grass some 5–6 m (5–6 yd) distant, invariably returning with a grasshopper held kicking and struggling in its beak. These grasshoppers were highly cryptic and, at close quarters, in daylight, it was difficult to distinguish them from the grass. That this remarkable bird should seemingly have no problem in spotting them at such a range in poor light is a clear pointer to its greatly superior vision. The implications of this amazing visual ability, for the evolution and survival of cryptic butterflies, are clear.

Some birds have the ability to modify their behaviour through experiment in order to take advantage of a previously unavailable source of food. A Neotropical tanager, *Pipraeidea melanonota*, for example, manipulates the bodies of ithomiines and other distasteful aposematic butterflies like a tube of tomato paste, squeezing out and gobbling up the abdominal contents and thus presumably avoiding the noxious chemicals stored in the discarded remains. Similarly, great tits, *Parus major*, have perfected the art of neatly decapitating caterpillars so that they can extract and toss away, in this instance, the guts with their accompanying plant toxins.

The overwintering populations of the unpalatable eastern monarch butterfly in Central Mexico are heavily preyed upon by two species of birds. They have solved the toxological conundrum in two different ways, one behavioural, the other physiological. Black-backed orioles, *Icterus abeillei*, exploit the variation in the emetic properties of the butterflies, this being linked to the concentration of cardenolides in their tissues. Weakly emetic individuals are consumed almost in their entirety, whereas those which are more strongly emetic are stripped of their thoracic muscles and abdominal contents; the cuticle with its more concentrated toxins is discarded. Black-headed grosbeaks, *Pheucticus melanocephalus*, on the other hand, eat the complete body of each butterfly regardless of how emetic it is, and only the inedible wings are discarded. Tests on the grosbeaks have established that this bird is very resistant to the emetic effects of the monarch's cardenolide defences. However, a very high percentage of monarchs were quickly released immediately after capture without apparently being harmed. This may be an example of olfactory or taste discrimination exercised by the birds in the presence of other odious chemicals such as pyrrolizidine alkaloids. These birds were found to be responsible for the deaths of several hundred thousand monarchs each year at their Mexican overwintering roost.

This difference in the palatability spectrum of toxic butterflies, discussed earlier, may also be exploited productively by birds in situations very different from those prevailing in the densely crowded overwintering sites of the monarchs. For example, while I was in South Africa I spent just a single afternoon photographing a pair of beautiful paradise flycatchers, *Terpsiphone viridis*, which were feeding chicks in the nest. During the space of about three hours the parents made 14 visits to the nest to bring food. Of the dainty morsels stuffed into the gaping mouths of the youngsters, five were butterflies. Three of these were whites, probably a species of *Colias* or *Belenois*, while the other two were *Danaus chrysippus*, a species which is supposed to be protected by its toxic properties. The explanation for this seemingly unusual situation could relate to two factors prevailing at the time. Firstly, the birds were feeding young, not themselves. With a nest full of ravenous chicks it may be that the adults were spurred on at least to sample everything that could be caught without expending too much effort, even to the extent of taking butterflies that in their previous experience had proved unpalatable. Monarchs are leisurely fliers by comparison with many other butterflies and therefore present a relatively easy target to the agile flycatchers. With the broad palatability spectrum exhibited by these monarchs, there is a good chance that the industrious birds will sooner rather than later come across a palatable specimen.

The second explanation involves the climatic conditions in that area of Africa. My experiences occurred just after a long and severe drought had been broken by ample rainfall. Despite this, most invertebrates were still to be found in unusually low numbers and maybe it was this lack of

In times of stress, such as during breeding, birds may be more liable to sample food which in easier times would be left well alone. This female paradise flycatcher, *Terpsiphone viridis* (the name is derived from the gorgeous male) has just stuffed a plain tiger butterfly, *Danaus chrysippus*, down the gullet of her hungry youngster which proceeded to eat it without any apparent unpleasant effects. Such an ability to eat butterflies which are normally accepted as being distasteful and aposematic is probably explained by the palatability spectrum, with some danaine individuals being nastier than others. Photographed in Kruger National Park, South Africa.

alternative food that was promoting the monarch-sampling experiments in the flycatchers, enabling them to provide their hungry young with at least some form of protein. It thus seems at least possible that during the breeding season of their avian enemies, and after protracted droughts, which are such a frequent phenomenon in Africa, monarch butterflies and their many mimics may be under considerably increased predatory pressure.

The rather languid flight of many danaines is not typical of most butterflies whose erratic bobbing and weaving aerial manoeuvres classify them as difficult targets. In most cases birds are sufficiently hard pressed to glean adequate sustenance from an often hostile environment, at the same time avoiding their own enemies, without squandering precious time and energy in aerial gymnastics chasing errant butterflies. This may in fact explain the relative scarcity of strong flying, gaudy nymphalines in the average avian diet. Anyone who has ever watched a bird attempting to catch such a butterfly in flight will be left in no doubt as to the difficulties inherent in the exercise and the majority of birds simply give up after a few abortive lunges. The exceptions are, of course, birds such as the flycatchers, which specialise in the mid-air capture of their insect prey. The paradise flycatchers were able to provide three of the elusive whites for their young, and in the British Isles spotted flycatchers, *Musicapa striata*, often present large whites and small tortoiseshells to their hungry nestlings.

Among mammals, mice and shrews almost certainly play a part in controlling butterfly populations, preying particularly on larvae and pupae which are located by means of the highly developed mammalian sense of smell. Pupae of the European swallowtail butterfly are known to be heavily preyed upon by small mammals in Scandinavia, while in the American state of Virginia, mice (*Peromyscus sp.*) and shrews (*Blarina sp.*) frequently eat overwintering pupae of *Papilio glaucus* and *Battus philenor*. A number of rodents seem to be resistant to or tolerant of the heart poisons employed by butterflies and this may also be the case with some monkeys. In Costa Rica, for example, squirrel monkeys, *Saimiri sciurus*, have been seen gorging themselves on the highly aposematic, gregarious nymphs of certain large, rain-forest grasshoppers, without apparently developing any adverse symptoms. This implies that aposematic butterfly larvae may also be at risk. Anyone who has watched the extremely thorough way in which a group of monkeys methodically sifts through an area of the forest canopy for every vestige of edible matter, cannot but doubt that they must count as major predators of butterfly larvae and pupae.

There is, of course, one other 'predator' of butterflies, whose ever-increasing global impact is threatening not only the survival of single species but of whole eco-systems. The reference here is, of course, to human beings and the implications of their continued and accelerating destruction of the world's natural resources are so vast that they merit inclusion in the final chapter.

Chapter 9
Ecology and Distribution

Butterflies do not exist in isolation but form an integral part of a much larger assemblage of animals and plants which interact in a complex way to form a community. Communities vary greatly according to their geographical location and their extremes of temperature and rainfall, all of which exert a powerful influence on the nature of the vegetation on which the animal members are completely dependent. Thus butterflies inhabiting the relatively stable environment in a tropical rain forest, where temperature, rainfall and day-length vary only within very narrow margins throughout the year, are represented by an enormous range of species. This diversity is made possible, without the risk of unbridled, wasteful competition, by the large number of ecological niches available within the complex jigsaw of the forest and the variety of potential host-plant species typically present. However, richness in species is not necessarily reflected in richness in numbers of individuals, for a characteristic of these rain forests is the relatively small sample of each species which can be seen on the wing in any single period, so that no one species appears conspicuously abundant or dominant.

The situation may be rather different in areas of sub-tropical forest, which have wider fluctuations both in temperature and rainfall, with a marked and quite lengthy dry season. An area of such forest occurs in Sao Paulo State in Brazil where a census was made of the populations of five species of ithomiines, three of which, *Mechanitis lysimnia*, *M. polymnia* and *Hypothyris ninonia*, belong to the same tiger-striped mimicry complex. The population of the three co-mimics grew considerably during the rainy season, but this growth was interrupted during the dry winter months when the three species came together to form dense local aggregations. Of the others studied, it was found that population growth of *Dircenna dero*, a non-aggregating species, took place mainly in autumn and winter, while *Mcclungia salonina* increased its numbers during summer and early winter, with a fall again in late winter and spring.

I observed a similar situation regarding the tiger-striped complex when I spent ten days in an area of seasonal forest at Fazenda Montes Claros in Minas Geraes State in Brazil. Arriving at the very end of the dry season, I found considerable aggregations of *Mechanitis lysimnia* and *M. polymnia* in very localised areas, their preferred sanctuary being dank, gloomy gullies, where the humidity was far higher than in the rest of the baking, tinder-dry, almost leafless forest. Two further Mullerian members of the tiger-striped complex were also present but in far smaller numbers. They were the larger and rather splendid ithomiine *Melinaea egina* and the danaine *Lycorea cleobaea cleobaea* (= *L. ceres*), while the pierid *Dismorphia amphione*, a presumed Batesian mimic of the others, lurked anonymously among its multitudinous models.

The same two species of *Mechanitis* foregathered in similar profusion along the humid, shady streamsides in sub-tropical gallery forest near Brasilia, a considerable distance away. Other members of the same complex were present as odd individuals, but the two usual heliconine members, *Heliconius eithila* and *Eueides isabella* were noticeable by their absence over a period of a week, although a local lepidopterist assured me that they were often to be seen on the wing in some numbers. This, therefore, raises the possibility that during the prolonged dry season the two species of *Mechanitis* fly the aposematic flag by themselves, the year-round availability of their distinctive colour-pattern obliging them to act as the central models for the rest of the mimicry complex, including the heliconiines, until summer arrives.

Even greater fluctuations in population densities are normal in temperate countries such as the British Isles and in deserts. In the British Isles, with its unpredictable climate, wide swings of the pendulum in butterfly populations are common, for numbers are controlled by climatic factors which influence their food and nectaring plants, the time available for mating and egg-laying and the activities of predators and parasites. Thus in some years caterpillars of the marsh fritillary, *Euphydryas aurinia*, swarm in near plague proportions in the damp, open, grassy rides in a wood near my home. Here, they envelop the vegetation in swathes of silk, to be followed a few weeks later by legions of adults basking on the oak leaves and feeding at the woodland flowers. Such a season of reproductive prosperity is often followed by a population crash and marsh fritillaries are then seldom seen for a few years, either as larvae or adults. Weather is probably a critical factor in these typical fluctuations in marsh fritillary populations, possibly acting in conjunction with the butterfly's parasites in the following way.

During a spring blessed with frequent clear skies, but suffering from generally low temperatures induced by northerly winds, the marsh fritillary caterpillars raise their temperature and shorten their development time by indulging in a considerable amount of basking. The overwintered pupae of their parasite, the tiny wasp *Apanteles bignellii*, are, however, hidden among grasses where the sun cannot penetrate and when the adult female wasps finally emerge, they discover that the butterfly caterpillars have beaten them to it and pupated. This ensures a large hatch of adult butterflies later in the year and, if all goes well, an even larger population of caterpillars in the following year. In a generally warm spring, on the other hand, the wasps hatch in synchrony with the caterpillars, resulting in a high level of parasitism, fewer adults and possibly a smaller population of caterpillars the next year.

No doubt there are numerous other factors involved as well, such as over-exploitation of the available host plant in favourable years, but the above example does serve to illustrate how apparently simple climatic factors can have a considerable knock-on effect on animal populations. Particularly unfavourable winters probably also have an effect by reducing the numbers of overwintering stages, with adverse effects on the size of early broods, but this may be reversed in later broods or in the following year, due to reduced levels of parasitism if the parasitoids too were hit by the bad winter. Also, the necessity of more extended search-times to locate the scarce and scattered hosts after a bad winter reduces the opportunities available for the parasitoids to lay their eggs. Food plant recovery during poor butterfly years is also a factor permitting rapid population growth in subsequent seasons, while in dry areas absence of nectaring sources for maintaining essential reproductive activity in adult butterflies can also be a major cause of decline in numbers.

Failure of the normal rainfall in a desert environment can have such a major effect on nectaring sources that a period of adult flight is more or less precluded and, in a succession of abnormally dry years, few butterflies will be on the wing; others may simply leap-frog the unfavourable conditions in a state of pupal diapause. Other species cope with the sporadic nature of desert rainfall patterns by migrating rapidly into areas favoured by recent precipitation, arriving at a suitable moment to cash in on the bounty of tender young leaves as the vegetation bursts into growth.

The northern tundras are basically unfriendly environments to sun-loving insects such as butterflies and only a few species manage to eke out an existence during the brief summer interludes, often needing two years to complete their life-cycles. Even in the tropics the higher mountains provide a habitat which, at almost any time of the year, is intrinsically hostile to such fragile insects as butterflies, due to the extremes of climate. Nevertheless, a number of particularly hardy butterflies are invariably present. For example, in the high Andes of Bolivia the winter days are pleasantly sunny and warm, while the nights become bitterly cold as temperatures plunge to well below freezing. Much of the bleak landscape is windswept and arid and the vegetation consists mainly of cacti along with tough dwarf herbs and wiry grasses. Winter rainfall is usually totally absent and the plant-life suffers accordingly, even the succulent cacti becoming shrivelled and dormant. This lengthy dry period is broken by occasional spells of springtime rains, when temperature and host plants are both sufficiently favourable to permit a rapid blossoming of butterfly activity in species such as the pierids *Tatochila xanthodice* and *Colias cesonia*. This is truncated, or at least severely reduced, by the violent arrival of the true summer rains, which then hold sway for two or three months. Considering the parched aspect of the landscape and the xerophytic nature of the vegetation, it seems surprising that it can rain without interruption for a month or more, the deluge gradually nibbling away at the barren hillsides until they subside in rivers of mud. The cacti sit sullenly in pools of silty water and the constant chill in the air restricts or prohibits any kind of butterfly activity for long periods. Remember this is summer! The local name for this particular season, however, is a more realistic summation of the prevailing gloom, for this summertime downpour is called *el invierno Boliviano*, the 'Bolivian winter'.

Natural extinctions of butterfly populations resident in reasonably favourable and stable environments are probably rare, except when occasioned by some catastrophic event such as a volcanic eruption (see below) or an assault by bulldozers. Survival is, however, less predictable in seasonally 'difficult' environments, such as mountain tops or deserts, where cyclic extinctions and recolonisations may be quite commonplace. A population's slide into oblivion may be precipitated by a variety of factors; for instance an unseasonal snowstorm in an area of the USA obliterated all of the available host plants at a critical stage in the life-cycle of the lycaenid, *Glaucopsyche lygdamus*, and sent its population over the brink. Similarly, the prolonged drought during the summer of 1976 was probably the final event which tipped the scales against the survival of the remaining population of the British large blue butterfly, a species vulnerable to such a climatic *coup de grâce* because of its short flight period. Other causes of extinction are more difficult to attribute, as for example in the population of the American fritillary, *Euphydryas editha*, which became extinct in 1964, was re-established in 1966 and then disappeared again in 1974. The highest population density ever achieved during this period was around 200 individuals, a total which is possibly below the threshold for successful survival through unfavourably dry seasons. In this example, the building up of larger numbers, capable of seeing the species through the bad times, was probably hindered by a scarcity of suitable nectaring sources.

Apocalyptic phenomena such as volcanic eruptions obviously have a devastatingly immediate outcome by obliterating all plant and animal communities within the immediate neighbourhood, the total impact decreasing with increasing distance from the centre of the eruption. The ecological effects resulting from such an event are currently being studied, centred around the catclysmic explosion in 1980, when Mount St Helens in America's Washington State underwent a dramatic self-annihilation. This covered an area of 200,000 sq km (77,220 sq miles) in a moderate to heavy ash fall which formed an impervious, choking mantle over the surrounding vegetation. Butterflies of several species were observed the following year in areas of moderate ash fall, albeit in reduced numbers. The ability to survive the destruction apparently depended on a number of factors, including the developmental state in which the butterfly's population found itself at the time of the eruption. Adults were seemingly especially vulnerable, larvae less so, although this again may have depended on the leaf texture of the host plant, shiny-surfaced leaves shedding ash more rapidly and thoroughly than those with hairy surfaces. Grasses rapidly slough off a coating of ash, so that grass-feeding satyrines were less severely affected.

Interestingly enough, repeated volcanic eruptions may even have promoted steps towards speciation in butterflies, by isolating populations

The Bolivian altiplano can be a hostile environment for butterflies, with extreme swings in the climate from very dry to torrentially wet, coupled with frequent low temperatures. A number of hardy species, such as *Colias (Zerene) cesonia*, do, however, manage to cope successfully with their difficult environment. Photographed at Oruro, Bolivia at 4,300 m (14,000 ft).

of sedentary species. Their members were unable to cross the extensive tracts of dry and barren ash and pumice deposits which separated the surviving isolated islands of vegetation, forming a kind of volcanic archipelago. Conversely, however, certain butterfly species are suited to colonising these newly created landscapes. Repeated volcanism has probably led to the evolution of the so-called 'Sand Creek-type' of the American fritillary, *Speyeria egleis*, whose present-day distribution corresponds closely to the fields of ash and pumice deposited by volcanoes in Oregon's Cascade mountains.

A catastrophic natural phenomenon which occurs more often is fire and it is such a regular component of the natural system in some areas that many species of plants and animals, indeed complete ecosystems, are dependent upon routine conflagrations for their maintenance. Such communities are common in Western Australia, where the intrinsic nature of the eucalyptus forests and sandplain vegetation is gradually altered if fire is rigorously excluded by man. Many plants will only burst into bloom after a bush fire, while others require the infernal caress of the flames to split open their woody seed pods, releasing the seeds therein. The resident butterflies are therefore dependent on fire to maintain a steady supply of host and nectaring plants and to clear the ground of the clutter of dead, smothering plant material which swiftly accumulates when fire is excluded. In North America it is the prairies which are adapted to withstand the periodic ravages of fires as the means of interrupting the natural progression of these areas towards a climax of woodland vegetation. A number of skippers and other butterflies rely upon these conflagrations to maintain and regenerate the open nature of their prairie grassland habitat.

In overcrowded Britain, with its intensively cultivated landscape, the maintenance of open grasslands for butterflies is sometimes difficult, since fire tends to be a socially unacceptable method of control. If applied with care, grazing animals are the perfect substitute and they have the advantage of being far more controllable than fire, as well as providing a useful end-product. I observed a good example of careful management using controlled grazing, which took place in a newly created nature reserve in the Cotswold Hills. Twenty years before its aquisition as a reserve the area had been a sheep pasture, well known as a habitat for a variety of lycaenids, but grazing was discontinued and it rapidly became overgrown with rank grasses and incipient scrub. These were gradually choking the short, sheep-nibbled turf, which had always been noted for its rich variety of dwarf wildflowers, valuable in themselves as well as providing the host and nectaring plants for the desirable lycaenids. The only butterflies present by the time the nature reserve was formed were several satyrines which prefer areas of long grass, although the inevitable progression to scrub would eventually have eliminated these as well. The management plan entailed dividing the whole reserve into plots with the introduction of a rotational grazing regime, which would gradually benefit the lycaenids and their food plants but would leave certain areas virtually untouched to maintain a habitat for the satyrines. After three or four years of this recipe the transformation was impressive and much of the grassland was already restored to its former glory as a fertile habitat for flowers and butterflies.

The enormous influence exerted by the height and density of the vegetational cover is particularly marked in woodlands through which man has cut broad swathes as rides. The resulting increase in sunlight along these rides promotes an exuberant growth of wild flowers, which provide a correspondingly wide range of sources of food for adult and larval butterflies. An open ride through mixed woodland in southern England will usually support a variety of nymphalines, satyrines, pierids, lycaenids and hesperids, whereas the undisturbed gloom of the neighbouring woodland may merely yield the odd speckled wood perched in a patch of sunlight.

In the tropics, the exigencies of life under a glaring sun often promote the reverse of the above situation. In the centre of Brazil, for example, lies a vast area known as the 'cerrado', a rolling landscape of sunny, open grasslands, gnarled shrubby trees and tangled low woodland, which is very difficult to penetrate on foot (*cerrado* means closed). Here and there small streams wend their way through the huge open tracts, their courses outlined from afar by the localised development of a humid, sub-tropical forest known as gallery forest. Frequently, this may extend for only 30 m (33 yd) or so on either side of the stream, where it provides sinuous arteries funnelling the pulsating animal life of the moist tropical forest through the sprawling expanses of sun-drenched grasslands.

Stepping into a belt of gallery forest in the open cerrado near Brasilia, one is, in a sense, transported instantly around 1,500 km (930 miles) away to one of the sub-tropical forests near Rio, or to Amazonia. The sun-loving lycaenids and pierids, typical of the open grassland, are abruptly replaced by the scintillating blue of a male morpho flapping unhurriedly along the stream, occasionally swooping down to investigate a shining leaf for signs of a suspected female. A second flash of blue, of a different shade, and a *Prepona* hurries past, while the fragrant clusters of flowers hanging from a nearby bush are gently fanned by the shivering

In South American rain forests a variety of butterflies haunts the gloomier spots on the forest floor. Perhaps the most characteristic of these are the glasswing satyrines such as this *Callitaera polita* feeding on a fallen fruit in lowland rain forest at Finca La Selva, Costa Rica.

wings of hosts of black and red *Parides* swallowtails. The tiger-striped brigades of ithomiines and their mimics are much in evidence, in the humid shade along the very edges of the streams. They often seem to be indulging in games of aerial tag or follow-my-leader as three or four of them chase one another, sometimes drifting down within reach of the spray from the tumbling, gurgling waters. In the very darkest spots lurk the 'transparents', ithomiines which shun the sunlight and purposefully seek the anonymity of the forest's perpetual gloom. These and innumerable other butterflies are accompanied by a veritable menagerie of exotic beetles, bugs and other insects typical of rain forests. Although the total faunal wealth is inferior to that of true rain forest, nevertheless it does represent one of the most remarkable examples I have seen of the abrupt differences generated by sudden change in habitat and ecology. Moreover, the South American continent is rich in such examples; for instance in Venezuela it is possible to go from a highly arid coastline dominated by thorny scrub and candelabra cacti, a habitat poor in butterflies, to a lush tangle of wet, tropical forest, haunted by morphos and owl butterflies, within a few kilometres!

Light and humidity are often the main factors influencing the ecology of butterflies and their host plants and the importance of these is manifest even within a single environment, such as a tropical rain forest. Here, the change in species occurs not so much as one walks through the forest but more as one looks up through the leafy canopy, for it is vertical stratification which influences the distribution of plants and animals in the relatively closed and stable environment of the mature forest. Little of the sun's radiation manages to penetrate as far as the ground, so that the vegetation at this level is often remarkably sparse and usually fails miserably to conform to the impenetrable maze of tangled vines and lianas inevitably encountered by macho celluloid heroes as they hack their way through it, their flashing machetes gleaming with sap.

In South America, the glasswing satyrines, such as *Haetera piera* and various species of *Cithaerias*, along with a multitude of ithomiines and heliconiines, are the most obvious tenants of the forest's ground-floor accommodation. On the other hand, many of the large and splendid swallowtails and showy nymphalines, so beloved of collectors, soar exuberantly way up out of reach in the lofty canopy, with its fecund 'gardens' of epiphytic plants flowering prolifically in the airy sunlight. Females of many butterfly species can seldom be tempted earthwards, spending the whole of their lives among the tossing treetops, although their males are driven earthwards by their desire to puddle or sample an offering of fresh animal droppings. The earthbound lepidopterist may therefore spend a surprising amount of time gazing upwards through binoculars, an occupation not without its hazards as I discovered in Costa Rica, when an enraged spider monkey forthrightly displayed its objection to my presence by pelting me with sticks and leaves, an unmistakable gesture whose message was backed up by a well-aimed shower of urine.

Butterflies are not distributed evenly over the land areas of the earth's surface but, in common with many other organisms, show a considerable increase in the number of species as the equator is approached. The harsh tundra of Greenland is able to provide board and lodging for only five species of stalwart butterflies, while the tropical country of Peru manages to boast no fewer than 4,000 or more species, mostly concentrated in the lush, rain forest areas to the east of the Andes. This is despite Peru having large areas of almost sterile desert set below soaring mountain ranges, habitats which are poor in butterflies. Nearer home, Bernwood Forest in southern England is a 400 hectare (988 acre) mosaic of woodland, which collectively comprises the richest single area in Britain for butterflies, boasting a total of 42 species, including a number of national rarities. Though rich by British standards, this hardly bears comparison with the Tambopata Natural Reserve in the Madre de Dios area of Peru, which consists of 5,500 hectares (13,590 acres) of virgin lowland tropical rain forest. Although butterfly-recording on the reserve is by no means complete, the list to date has reached the staggering total of 1,122 species! This figure is greatly in excess of the total number of butterfly species found in the combined land areas of North America and Europe!

Britain has been gravely afflicted by successive glaciations, which have done much to reduce its faunal wealth, and most of Europe and North America has been similarly affected. However, the traumatic glacial events which are partly responsible for much temperate faunal impoverishment may actually have played a pivotal role in the evolution of the impressively rich faunal diversity, including butterflies, found in Amazonia. Repeated glaciations in the temperate regions have probably produced radical changes in the climate over Central Brazil, creating long, dry periods which favoured the retreat of the tree cover into forested islands surrounded by seas of sun-baked grasslands. Each island would possess its own ecological peculiarities which would tend to encourage the evolution of sub-species and species within the community. At the same time, out-breeding with members of the same species from other neighbouring communities would be hindered or prevented by the reluctance or inability of the shade-loving forest dwellers to cross the intervening areas of glaring, windswept grassland. This theory is a direct contradiction of earlier ideas which proposed that the high faunal diversity was due to the great 'stability' of the forests over thousands of years, thus providing a continuous and uninterrupted period during which evolution could take place.

Dispersal in butterflies

Sooner or later adverse changes in a butterfly's habitat, such as depletion of its host plants or nectaring sources, severe local overcrowding, the approach of winter, or a prolonged dry season, may elicit an urge to leave the place of its birth and seek pastures new. Apart from the well-researched examples concerning the spectacular migrations of the American monarch butterfly (see below), relatively little detailed work

The gorgeous nymphalid *Nessaea ancaeus ancaeus* is but one of more than 1,100 species of butterfly recorded in the Tambopata Natural Reserve, an area of 5,500 hectares (13,590 acres) of tropical lowland rain forest in Peru. This individual is in particularly pristine condition, and has probably only recently hatched.

has been carried out into the mechanisms and motivations of migration, and the work so far undertaken has sometimes led to curiously incompatible results. Thus one set of researchers concluded that, on average, adult small whites, *Pieris rapae*, died at no distance greater than 2 km (1 mile) from their birthplace, while another researcher has concluded that the final resting place of the average small white was at a distance of no less than 200 km (124 miles) from its place of origin: quite a discrepancy!

Remarkably compact colonies are formed by some butterflies, often tied to a particular food plant which itself may require a special type of soil or a specific stage in a seral succession. Thus in Britain, the distribution of the small blue, *Cupido minimus*, is closely linked with the distribution of the food plant, a dwarf legume, which prefers south-facing calcareous slopes where the plant succession has been interrupted by grazing or fire, thereby maintaining a short grass sward. However, the food plant occurs in many localities from which the small blue is absent, probably indicating the basically sedentary nature of the females. Alternatively, it may relate to the inability of the females to locate widely scattered and very localised colonies of the food plant or to other small but important differences in the habitat where the latter grows. Some butterflies do indeed exhibit a remarkable ability to pinpoint areas which constitute a suitable habitat, even when these consist of tiny oases in wide expanses of country otherwise unsuited to colonisation.

I recently took a walk near my childhood home in Gloucestershire, sadly lamenting the many changes for the worst which had taken place since I had walked that way in my youth. The fields and copses had

The scintillating satyrine *Caeruleuptychia glauca* is but one of more than 1,100 species of butterfly recorded from the Tambopata Natural Reserve, an area of 5,500 hectares (13,590 acres) of lowland tropical rain forest in Peru. The dubious reputation enjoyed by most 'browns' for being drably coloured is not reflected in this metallic blue species, one of many brilliantly coloured satyrines found in the Neotropical region.

been completely wiped out and replaced by the urban desert of a light industrial estate, which even today is creeping irrevocably outwards, strangling the countryside and its wildlife in a concrete grip. Imagine my surprise then, when a marbled white butterfly suddenly flew across my path, for in Gloucestershire this species is almost always restricted to the Cotswold Hills where it is usually found on downland slopes with areas of long grass growing above the underlying limestone rock. This particular butterfly had fluttered across a fence which bounded a small area of wasteland left untouched to one side of the encroaching factories. Further investigation established that a pond, which both of us have known since we were children, had formerly occupied this much-changed area and had at some time been filled in with oolite limestone brought down from the neighbouring Cotswolds. Typical calcium-loving plants, such as the precious little bee orchid, *Ophrys apifera*, had become well established, possibly from seeds brought in with the limestone spoil. It is exceedingly doubtful, however, that the marbled whites could have arrived by the same route and it seems indisputable that they had made their way to this isolated spot under their own volition. It would appear that some wandering female, persistently prospecting for likely habitats, had located this parcel of land, a mere 15 × 20 m (16 × 22 yd) in size, and had recognised its suitability for the laying of her precious egg-batch.

In the San Francisco area of the USA the food plant utilised by the butterfly *Euphydryas editha* is, these days, found only on serpentine soils. Colonies of the butterfly in these areas are relatively stable but in the absence of adequate nectar supplies for the adults, there is evidence that there is a greater tendency for dispersal, especially among females. Even within a colony, when host plants and nectaring sources are widely separated, dispersal may take place locally on a daily basis. In a canyon in the Inner Coast Range of California, *E. editha* utilises a host plant (a *Pedicularis sp.*) which grows only along the ridge tops; late in the flight season nectar sources can only be found in bloom along the creek at the bottom of the canyon, forcing the adult butterflies to undertake a daily vertical migration in order to survive. By way of contrast, adult marbled whites in Britain do not need to vacate a favoured nectar source in order to lay their eggs, for these can simply be dropped into the grass below.

Special problems face those butterflies which exploit an ephemeral food plant which is present in an area for only a brief period before it is replaced by a stronger growing competitor. Individuals of *Papilio polyxenes* in Costa Rica disperse continuously in order to exploit the brief period of suitability of their larval food plant, *Spananthe paniculata*. Females set off in search of a fresh patch of this plant as soon as they have underwritten the future of at least a handful of their progeny by laying a batch of eggs on the steadily deteriorating food plant on which they themselves were nourished.

A latent inability or unwillingness to traverse an area of unsuitable habitat may also lead to a restriction in range, even though the butterfly may be perfectly capable of surviving and breeding successfully in an area far removed from its normal home. A colony of *Euphydryas gillettii* was successfully established in Colorado, USA from eggs and larvae transplanted from its normal home in Wyoming. The success of this colonisation established that the absence of this species from Colorado could be accounted for by its reluctance or inability to cross the lowland gap in the Rocky Mountains formed by the Wyoming Basin. Even within a small country, such as England, species may be very localised for no apparent reason. The Glanville fritillary, *Melitaea cinxia*, is, for example, known only from a very specialised habitat found along the undercliff on the Isle of Wight. Such a restriction to a specialised habitat would seem to indicate that a micro-climate found only at the base of these chalk cliffs is vital for the survival of this species. Yet a colony has been successfully introduced into the Cotswold Hills, some 160 km (100 miles) distant, where it occupies a very different micro-climate. Almost the only factor in common with its normal home is the calcareous nature of the underlying rock and the existence of abundant host and nectaring plants.

Why some butterflies are regular wanderers and rapidly colonise new areas, while others seem disinclined to move more than a few metres from their birthplace, remains a mystery. However, mating strategies may be a significant factor, for butterflies such as *Euphydryas* have a genital plugging device, preventing further matings even if they do disperse. Nomadic butterflies, such as *Colias*, on the other hand, court and mate several times, making dispersal a more reasonable investment for future breeding success.

Population densities may also affect the likelihood of dispersal, though little concrete information is available on actual numbers of individuals. In the British Isles, butterflies such as the adonis, common and chalk-hill blues, marbled white and meadow brown may all reach very high densities in favourable years. High alpine populations of *Euphydryas anicia* in the USA have been estimated to attain peaks of 100,000 individuals, while *Lycaena epixanthe* has been recorded in densities of tens of thousands per hectare (2.5 acres) in the pine barrens of New Jersey. The availability of a food plant within only a restricted area obviously tends to concentrate numbers, whereas butterflies utilising a more widespread host plant, e.g. many of the grass-feeding Satyrinae, may be more scattered. In densely populated regions of the world, such as the British Isles, it is the severe restrictions on the areas of suitable habitat imposed by human activities which often result in high population densities. Overcrowding may lead to saturation of larval food plants and adult nectaring sources, with a consequent likelihood of dispersal in search of more favourable areas. Indeed, in *Pieris protodice* it was found that the females were actually encouraged to disperse because of unremitting harassment by an excess of frustrated males.

While many species of butterflies are remarkably sedentary or disperse only under special conditions which may not occur every year, certain species are regular migrants. Every year painted ladies, *Vanessa cardui*, migrate northwards through Europe from their breeding areas in North Africa and southern Europe. The actual distance covered by any one

While some butterflies, such as the painted lady, *Vanessa cardui*, are habitual arrivals in the British Isles from continental breeding areas, the arrival on British soil of certain other species is a cause for considerable celebration among endemic lepidopterists. Such an occasional but most welcome migrant is the queen of Spain fritillary *Issoria lathonia* seen here feeding on a knapweed flower in central France.

The clouded yellow, *Colias croceus*, is a regular migrant to the British Isles from continental Europe, but it is only at intervals of a few years that this butterfly arrives in sufficient numbers for it to be easily seen throughout the country. This is a male feeding on a knapweed, one of the favoured Asteraceae which provides abundant nectar in multiple florets. Photographed in Warwickshire, England.

The pierid *Belenois aurota* is a noted migrant, following the rains in semi-arid areas of southern Africa, thereby taking full advantage of the newly burgeoning vegetation. In April 1984 this species was present in large numbers in the Kalahari in South Africa, and clusters of puddling butterflies were invariably present on the margins of the waterholes provided for the big game. Three days later they were all gone.

individual is not currently known, for breeding also takes place en route and the resultant progeny also continue the northwards flight.

The pierid *Belenois aurota* is a noted migrant which flies eastwards through southern Africa in December and January, basically following the pattern of rainfall occurring in arid areas. When I was in the Kalahari Desert in South Africa one late March, this butterfly was migrating through in countless thousands, settling in dense swarms to drink on the damp, mineral-saturated sand bordering the waterholes provided for the big game.

In North America the most famous migrant is of course the monarch, and the long years of painstaking work by Dr Fred Urquhart and his team, which finally led them to the winter roosts of millions of eastern monarchs in the cool mountains of Mexico's Michoacan State, is one of the classic biological detective stories of recent times. Methodical tagging of individuals was a vital aid to the discovery of the roosts and also conveyed a great deal of information about the routes taken and what happens to the butterflies during their migration. It was learned, for example, that most males die as they press northwards from Mexico, while some butterflies were found to cover as much as 130 km (81 miles) in a single day's flying. Distinct variations in the physical condition of monarchs captured during the summer in Ontario suggested that overlapping generations arrive in Canada, battered specimens having, in most instances, undertaken the long journey from the south; those arriving in good condition having hatched more recently at some intermediate point on the migration route to the north. As the northern winter draws nearer and the days shorten, the females of the latest broods fail to develop productive ovaries, setting off southwards as virgins to mature sexually as they roost in their millions among the mountain pines. Months pass before they once again feel the urge, as spring arrives, to return northwards, mating and reproducing as they go. The monarch's choice of a mountainous site in which to overwinter seems to be dictated by temperature, which hovers around freezing point for long periods, ideal conditions for conserving energy and making the most efficient use of valuable food reserves.

Chapter 10
Butterflies and Man

State of play – the tropics

The relationship between mankind and butterflies is currently going through a particularly distressing phase as human exploitation of the planet, with little regard for the long-term outcome, leads to constantly escalating destruction and degradation of every kind of butterfly habitat around the world. Even remote areas of deserts and mountains are increasingly being opened up to the deleterious, long-lasting effects of overgrazing by goats and the elimination of forests for firewood and agriculture. Much of this is a result of human access being facilitated by the increasing tendency of Third World countries to drive roads into previously inaccessible areas, projects which are usually only possible because of finance provided by the developed world.

The possibly tragic and certainly sad consequences of continuing to fell the world's remaining tropical forests, at the present rate, are so well known by now that I scarcely need to dwell on them here, except perhaps to remind the reader that the greater part of the world's butterfly population is restricted to these forests which are losing an area equivalent to half the size of Britain each year. For example, unless there are radical changes at governmental level, prognostications indicate that little natural tropical rain forest will remain in the Far East by the end of the century. The determined attempts currently (1987) being made by some of the indigenous tribes in Malaysian Borneo's forests to stop, by physical force if necessary, the relentless advance of the logging companies bent on destroying their millenia-old ecosystem, is a welcome sign that some people at least are willing to stand up for their future. The situation has not been helped by the West's burgeoning demand for tropical timbers and agricultural products, the latter having led to vast areas of natural forest being obliterated in favour of monocultural plantations of oil palm, coffee or tea.

Some countries favour ranching and when visiting Costa Rica in 1986 I was depressed to discover that within the previous ten years the bulk of the country's lowland tropical rain forest, and much of its hill forest as well, had been converted into pasture. Most of this was of such poor quality that it would have been sneered at by the average European farmer and what had been, until so frustratingly recently, one of the world's richest and most diverse habitats was now just a huge hamburger factory. The most ironic part of this affair is the published figures showing a decline in meat consumption in Costa Rica during the period when most of the land was devastated for cattle rearing. This may seem a puzzling contradiction until one realises that the majority of the meat is for export. (This all happened during a period when the 'beef mountains' were piling up in Europe.)

While the past situation in Costa Rica is distressing, at least the future seems rather brighter, especially for a Third World country. By the mid-1990s the government, which now has an outstanding commitment to conservation, aims to have set aside the majority of the remaining natural areas as National Parks, as well as hoping to reafforest areas already degraded by many years of overgrazing by cattle. Watershed management is also considered a priority and in future this may be one of the most important ways of persuading Third World governments to conserve highland forests for butterflies and other wildlife. The superb Guatopo National Park in Venezuela is on a watershed supplying water to Caracas, so it is highly unlikely that any future pressure from logging or agricultural interests will persuade the government to de-gazette the area, as unfortunately happened recently in a number of Asian parks after commercial pressure was brought to bear.

Unfortunately, the crippling burden of debt incurred by so many of these poorer countries may, at the last moment, encourage unwise short-term exploitation of natural resources, just as many of them are becoming aware of the ecological problems likely to approach if development is allowed to proceed unchecked. On the credit side, the growing level of tourism from developed countries can do much to persuade Third World governments to view conservation in a favourable light. Consequently, readers of this book, who have dreamed of experiencing the thrill of watching butterflies and other animals in a tropical forest, are strongly urged to take the plunge and go! Ensure, however, that the tourist office of the country concerned is well aware that it is the butterflies and other wildlife in the forests that have tempted you to spend your precious tourist dollars there and not merely the glittering beaches, colourful carnivals and multifarious other attractions. All governments are susceptible to national economic pressures, as well as to complaints from local people that habitat conservation loses them money. The off-the-beaten-track kind of tourism enjoyed by butterfly enthusiasts is just the sort of thing needed to tip the scales in favour of conservation over development. It also has the advantage of bringing long-term benefits to the local community via the money spent in nearby towns and villages and in wages to rangers and local guides. An expanding series of well-organised 'butterfly safaris' would certainly be helpful in supporting and encouraging the concept of rain forest conservation in many countries, especially in those where the more obviously appealing 'cuddly' animals, such as monkeys and chimps, are not present to stimulate local and international interest and sympathy.

It has to be said that there is nothing quite so alluring as dollar

The fabulous Guatopo National Park is an area of superb tropical rain forest
originally established to protect the watershed supplying the main water
catchment area for Caracas, the capital city of Venezuela. One denizen, the
splendid owl butterfly, *Caligo atreus*, has a particularly striking underside. It is a
nymphalid belonging to the sub-family Brassolinae which is restricted to the
Neotropical region.

signs attached to a butterfly's wings to turn a government official's head and set bureaucratic knees a-tremble. The pecuniary approach to butterfly conservation has often been neglected, but not in Papua New Guinea, where the government realised some years ago that the country was in the fortunate position of having a natural, pollution-free, environmentally-safe product which is often, literally, worth more than its weight in gold; namely several species of *Ornithoptera* birdwing butterflies. International trade in wild-caught birdwings had escalated throughout the 1960s, mainly to the financial benefit of a few foreign-based dealers; then, in 1966, the government introduced the Fauna Protection Ordinance which declared complete protection for seven species of *Ornithoptera*. Concurrently the government's Division of Wildlife initiated the Insect Farming, Trading and Conservation Project, aimed at assisting rural people to set up butterfly farms, as well as carrying out research and environmental improvement programmes. A decade later, 500 butterfly farms had sprung up across the country, selling their products through a centralised governmental agency, to help satisfy the world demand for pinned butterflies, which currently runs at several million per year. This deluge is intended for a variety of customers, including specialist collectors, museums, students and the man in the street, who uses them as exotic decorations in the home. One of the great advantages of establishing such a butterfly farm lies in the very low initial cash investment needed, a significant factor in a Third World country.

A second advantage lies in the environmental benefits accruing from the lack of necessity to hack down the natural forest cover, the destructive prelude to planting more traditional cash-crops such as tea and rubber. Instead, the first step is merely to plant sufficient quantities of the required caterpillar food plant accompanied by favoured sources of nectar. Ensuring the maximum productivity involves a certain amount of extra effort, such as the transfer to rearing cages of leaves with eggs attached, where they are better protected from enemies, or the sleeving of branches in situ. Pupae attached within easy reach are carefully transferred to a protected hut and sprayed with water each evening to prevent desiccation. Pristine adults are killed and papered before spending a few days drying out on a basic drier consisting of sheets of black plastic. When sufficient specimens have accumulated, the farmer dispatches them in a specially designed cardboard box to the buying agency. Papua New Guinea has few roads and aircraft provide the sole lifelines to most areas, so with freight costs being correspondingly high, the ability to harvest a light-weight, high-value cash-crop such as butterflies is a significant fillip for rural communities. More recently, Malaysia has seen the construction of a very large and modern butterfly farm and it is possible that other countries will follow suit.

However, it has to be asked whether, despite the bad press that collecting in habitat increasingly receives, it would not also be a good idea to impress upon Third World governments that commercial collecting of butterflies could be one of a variety of ways of establishing integrated programmes for the long-term sustainable harvesting of forest products? This would be a direct replacement for the irredeemable policy of clear-felling for momentary gain, or slashing and burning for agricultural use, which is sustainable for only a limited period without inputs of large amounts of artificial fertiliser, impracticable for a Third World economy. Various organisations in the USA are currently involved in trying to persuade Latin-American governments to consider just this type of approach, which may hold more hope for the long-term future of butterflies and other forest fauna and flora than the establishment of National Parks and reserves. These, unfortunately, are often viewed with open hostility by local people faced with stark economic reality. As a high value crop, butterflies could play a central role in enabling areas of forest to provide sufficient capital return to persuade both governments and local residents that it is better to leave the trees in place, for the future benefit of themselves and their children, rather than raze them to the ground with potentially disastrous repercussions.

Had such a system been in place ten years ago, the government of Papua New Guinea might have thought twice about establishing the Popondetta Smallholder Oil Palm Development Project which necessitated felling a priceless section of the dangerously small area of forest inhabited by the world's largest, and one of its rarest, butterflies, Queen Alexandra's birdwing, *Ornithoptera alexandrae*. As one observer said resignedly to me when I was there, a single *alexandrae* is worth an awful lot of palm oil and is far less trouble to harvest and process. So perhaps research into this butterfly's ecological requirements, leading to increased populations via artificially provided food plants, might have proved a wiser investment than farming palm oil, a product which is currently (1987) falling in price due to a steadily growing world glut.

The Philippines is another country which in recent years has seen a rapid diminution in its rain forests, as much as 80 per cent of which has disappeared in the past ten years. This has had disastrous results not only for butterflies, but also for people who have seen their water supplies become polluted or disappear as erosion fills the rivers with silt. Some of the remaining species of butterflies are, however, now susceptible to extermination at the hands of unscrupulous commercial collectors. One example is *Papilio chikae* from northern Luzon, whose corpse is so valuable that just a few are needed to turn even a long-distance collecting trip from America or Japan into a profitable venture. Yet, by its very nature, this high value could be a saviour for the butterfly's habitat, for with such a very valuable commodity it would not require a very dramatic increase in productivity, perhaps via habitat enrichment, to transform its forest home into a sustainable source of income for the local people.

If the plight of the swallowtails as a family can be used as a measure of the problems facing butterflies worldwide, then the situation is somewhat alarming, for it is estimated that 61 (11 per cent) of the world's swallowtail species are threatened while the status of a further 111 (19 per cent) cannot be adequately assessed at present because of lack of data. Five Third World countries, China, Philippines, Indonesia, Brazil and Madagascar together play host to over half of the world's swallowtails; the inclusion of five more countries, Malaysia, Taiwan, Papua New Guinea, India and Mexico boosts the total to two-thirds. Targeting these countries for maximum efforts at butterfly conservation would therefore seem a wise move, at least in the short term.

State of play – temperate countries

It would be a boost to the ego to be able to say that the situation regarding the conservation of butterflies and their habitats in the wealthy, temperate world is superior to the situation prevailing in the underfinanced Third World. Alas, this is not the case, for the governments of many developed countries have a dismal conservation record and could learn much from a few Third World governments, such as that of Costa Rica. On occasions government-sponsored attempts at species conservation have possibly been well intentioned, but are so wide of the mark that one wonders whether they really are serious, or mere sops to public opinion. Thus the State Government of Queensland declared legal protection for the mountain blue, *Papilio ulysses*, and the two birdwings *Ornithoptera priamus* and *O. richmondia*. While making it illegal for anyone to collect these species, the government did little to ensure the future safety of the habitat vital for their continued survival and indeed was often the chief sponsor in promoting both logging of their forest homelands and damaging encroachments, such as the proposed road through the Daintree Forest area. Near Brisbane occur the only known localities for one of the world's rarest butterflies, Illidges's ant-blue, *Acrodipsas illidgei*, whose larvae and pupae lodge in the nests of tiny black *Crematogaster* ants in mangrove trees. This blue is known from only three areas of mangroves in Moreton Bay; one locality has already been destroyed by ill-conceived housing projects; one is in an area where there are plans for a canal-estate development; the third is not currently in danger but it is depressingly unlikely that this will remain the case for much longer in view of the previous history of the species. Saving the narrowly endemic Illidge's ant-blue from extinction is surely a far more worthy project than, say, the re-introduction of the widespread large blue into the British Isles and it deserves an equal amount of publicity and financing.

The situation in the USA is not a great deal better and what conservation of butterflies and other invertebrates has taken place has been effected largely by the efforts of the admirable, voluntarily funded Nature Conservancy, and more recently by the Xerces Society. The latter is named after the diminutive lycaenid *Glaucopsyche xerces*, an erstwhile inhabitant of dune areas near San Francisco and the first species of North American butterfly to be extirpated as a result of human encroachment. This society is involved in a number of praiseworthy conservation projects, including the aim of establishing the permanent protection of vital overwintering sites for the monarch butterfly both in California and in Mexico. One would have thought that all the over-

Big game safaris can also turn up a good deal of interesting small game, such as this sumptuous yellow pansy butterfly, *Precis hierta*. This nymphaline is a typical inhabitant of the savannah-woodland areas which have been set aside as reserves for the larger mammals. This individual was one of numerous butterflies feeding on a flowering bush in the Timbavati reserve in the Transvaal, South Africa.

wintering roosts in a developed country such as the USA would have been strictly protected for years; it may therefore come as a considerable surprise to many readers, as indeed it did to us, to learn that residential and business parks have often irreversibly modified the micro-environment vital to the monarchs, and developers have, in fact, obliterated a total of seven roosts in the last three years. Government officials were lamentably ignorant of the roosts' locations and how they should be managed to ensure their long-term survival.

Luckily, the situation is beginning to improve but there is still a long way to go before the US can match the measures quickly taken by its Third World neighbour, Mexico, in protection of its own vast roosts. This has involved an increasing amount of legal protection for the sites so that disturbance, especially logging and cutting for firewood, is restricted. At the same time snowballing public interest in the matchless spectacle presented by millions of monarch butterflies garlanding the trees like living confetti, has led to such an increase in visitors to the public roost at El Rosario (50,000 visitors in 1985–86, mostly Mexicans), that trampling by curious sightseers was beginning to pose a threat. A first-class interpretive centre has now been established and progress has been made in providing alternatives to wood-cutting as a way of life for local residents; money earned from booming tourism seems to be the most likely alternative, with the advantage of giving the locals a vested interest in the continued survival of the forest and its butterflies.

In the British Isles there has been a depressingly familiar decline in most butterfly species over the past 30 years, due to a number of factors, dominant among which have been the enormous changes in land use which have swept across the landscape since the Second World War. These have involved large-scale conversion of woodland and rough pasture to arable crops and improved grasslands almost devoid of butterflies. Much of this destruction has been wrought by the ploughing under of the habitats of rare butterflies in the British Isles' National Parks. In 1982, for example, the Ministry of Agriculture's 'wildlife advisers' pronounced that one of the richest wildflower sites in the North Yorks Moors National Park should be 'improved' with the aid of a government grant. The advisers were well aware that the site in question harboured one of the few remaining Yorkshire breeding colonies of the British Isles' sole riodinine, the Duke of Burgundy, *Hamaeris lucina*, a species in serious national decline. Yet the recommendation was warmly given to the farmer to go ahead and destroy both the wild flowers and the butterflies!

Fortunately the situation in the British Isles seems to be changing, both with regard to farming practices in general and to butterflies in particular. Farmers may now actually be encouraged by government departments to be mindful of, or even improve, habitats for wildlife, rather than going for all-out production. 'Butterfly Year' in 1981–82 (actually two years), sponsored by the British Butterfly Conservation Society, accompanied by the issue of beautiful commemorative stamps by the Post Office and by a great deal of publicity, did much to stimulate a heightened awareness of butterflies in the UK. This applies not only to the general public but also to the people running organisations dedicated to acquiring and maintaining nature reserves where invertebrates in general have been largely ignored during the process of selecting and managing reserves. This has sometimes had dire results, such as the depressing frequency of rapid declines to extinction which have occurred in many populations of the rarest British butterflies within a few years of reaping the 'benefit' of protection on a nature reserve. Inadequate or incorrect management stemming from insufficient understanding of the ecological requirements of a particular species has usually been the cause leading to these extinctions.

The greater importance now attached to butterflies since Butterfly Year, backed up by management techniques based more firmly on research carried out into the ecological requirements of the rarer species, is now paying off with some spectacular successes. Thus, in 1986, the Royal Society for the Protection of Birds proudly announced that a record 1,500 of one of the British Isles' rarest butterflies, the heath fritillary, *Mellicta athalia*, were on the wing in four colonies in one of its reserves in Kent. The fact that these were all flying in specially provided rides and glades was rewarding proof of the vital role played by previous research; this had established that the heath fritillary requires woodland with plenty of sunlight, preferably in an early successional stage or its equivalent.

Such essential knowledge came too late to save the last English colony of chequered skippers, *Carterocephalus palaemon*, which sank into oblivion almost before anyone noticed anything was amiss. The last colony existed on a nature reserve, where rides had been kept open and specially mown to keep the colonies thriving, yet they still became extinct. This was simply because no one had apparently noticed that the surrounding trees had, with time, outgrown the width of the rides, casting heavy shade with disastrous results for the butterfly. This species still thrives in a number of colonies in Scotland, a situation which was unsuspected until its extinction in England fostered an intense interest in its status north of the border.

Photographing butterflies in the field

A 35 mm single lens reflex camera is essential for any kind of wildlife work, as it can be accurately focused and will accept a variety of lenses of different focal lengths. The ideal lens for butterfly work is probably a 70–150 mm macro-zoom, which allows a greater working distance from your flighty subject than is possible with a standard 50 mm lens. The zooming facility is also useful for framing your subject to your requirements, once you are sufficiently close. An 80–210 mm zoom lens is also useful, but is rather larger and heavier, and 90 mm, 100 mm and 135 mm fixed focal length lenses can also be used to good effect, although with these, unless they are specific macro lenses, you will also have to purchase a set of extension tubes. This usually consists of three tubes, each different in length, which can be used singly or in any combination depending upon how close you wish to get to your subject. Extension tubes enable you to focus closer than the shortest distance marked on your lens.

If you wish to concentrate on photographing butterflies by available light, then you must ensure that your extension tubes have a device for coupling your lens to the through-the-lens (TTL) metering system on your camera. This enables the TTL meter to compensate for the light which is lost whenever extension tubes are mounted on the camera, as the automatic coupling allows the light to be measured with the lens aperture fully open. For close-ups of a butterfly's face or for batches of eggs, a standard 50 mm lens must be used, also mounted on extension tubes. A 50 mm lens on 50 mm of extension will enable you to take a life-size photograph of a butterfly's face, with its slender proboscis probing into a flower. If you wish, however, to get even closer, so that the image on the photograph will be magnified to greater than life-size, e.g. for close-ups of the intricate sculpturing on the surface of butterfly eggs, then it is preferable to mount the lens in a reversed position, i.e. with the front of the lens pointing towards the camera. This can easily be achieved by using a reversal ring screwed to the front of the lens, which is then mounted onto the extension tubes. This results in the loss of the automatic coupling to the lens diaphragm, but each camera manufacturer has its own device for operating the latter in the reversed position, e.g. on our own Nikons there is a ring which mounts onto the lens bayonet using a simple finger-operated plunger to activate the diaphragm.

Like most professionals we prefer to restrict our film stock to Kodachrome 64 with its outstanding colour stability and keeping properties, although this normally rules out the use of available light for photographing any insects other than pale-coloured butterflies on a bright day. This is because, to be on the safe side, it is preferable to use a shutter speed of at least 1/125th second when shooting with a hand-held camera, even when steadied by the use of a monopod (see below). Since Kodachrome 64 is relatively insensitive to light, being classed as a 'slow' film, using it on a sunny day in the British Isles for photographing a colourful butterfly would usually involve using 1/125th second at f8. This is quite a wide aperture, which restricts the depth of field, making very accurate positioning of the camera essential, so that the plane of focus runs from side to side across the wing area. Even so, a butterfly resting or feeding with its wings open would need to have them spread very flat, otherwise either the body or the wing tips will be out of focus. A shutter speed of 1/125th second is incapable of stopping much in the way of movement such as camera shake due to an unsteady hand, shaking of the plant due to wind or the natural movements of the feeding butterfly. However, switching to Kodachrome 200 enables a change to 1/250th second at f8/11 under the same lighting conditions, a considerable improvement all round.

Butterflies, however, do not spend the whole of their lives conveniently perched, virtually motionless, on flowers in bright sunlight on almost windless days and if you want good coverage of the richest assemblage of butterflies on earth, then you will have to adopt techniques which enable you to shoot in the gloomy depths of tropical forests. Even Kodachrome 200 may be of little use under these conditions and an electronic flash is obligatory for anyone wishing to obtain clear, well-focused pictures of their subjects. We have experimented with a variety of combinations for mounting flashes while using an 80–210 mm zoom lens and we finally settled on a system whereby a medium-size unit is mounted on a bar to one side of the camera, with a smaller flash mounted on the camera hot-shoe and acting as a source of fill-in illumination. This seems to give more sparkling results, especially for species with metallic markings, than having a flash mounted to each side of the camera, as direct frontal lighting seems to reflect back more intensely from interference colours than does angled lighting. You will have to take a number of test shots with this set-up, perhaps using pinned specimens for convenience, to establish the correct exposures for various sizes of butterflies and operating distances, jotting down the information for future reference.

Our twin flash set-up gives us an aperture of f16 for a fairly large butterfly, such as a *Papilio* sitting with wings outspread and shot at just under 1m (1 yd) from the lens. Some readers will have a camera with a TTL flash facility which automatically takes care of exposure problems, even when using multiple flash systems. These TTL systems should, however, be used with care; they will, for example, give perfect results every time for a gaudy nymphalid sitting with outspread wings on the dull rain forest floor or on a leaf, but will usually overexpose a similar-sized butterfly if white or yellow are the dominant colours. Similarly, a dark butterfly posed against a pale background will be underexposed. Generally speaking, however, TTL flash is an excellent method of facilitating quick and accurate coverage of the host of splendid butterflies which can be found feeding on muddy ground in the tropics, or at urine baits.

In temperate countries TTL flash tends to be less useful, as butterflies are often found feeding or perching on isolated flower-heads, surrounded by a lot of empty space. Under these commonplace circumstances the camera's sensor will be misled by the relatively small amount of light reflected from the subject, because most of the light whizzes off past it and disappears into thin air. Overexposure is the inevitable result and we prefer to use our manual flashes with bracketed exposures, i.e. one picture at the exposure we think by experience to be the correct one, one at ½ stop less and one at ½ stop more.

Bracketing is always to be recommended, especially where a subject is willing to sit around and let you take a series of pictures. For close-ups of butterfly faces or eggs we use a small manual flash held in the left hand, which gives a more or less consistent exposure of f16 on Kodachrome 64. A ring flash, especially with TTL facility, makes life very easy for real close-ups, particularly if you make the light a little less flat and uninteresting by blocking off part of the ring with dark tape.

Butterflies need to be stalked with great care, as they are extremely sensitive to movement. Some species are particularly jittery and almost impossible to photograph and here the male orange-tip, *Anthocharis carda-mines*, comes immediately to mind. Others such as a peacock, *Nymphalis io*, busily probing buddleia flowers, or a *Charaxes* boozing on fermenting fruit, are relatively easy and can be photographed with a 50 mm lens. Time of day and weather conditions also play a part and butterflies which have consistently proved impossible to approach for several days may suddenly become almost tame, often for no apparent reason. Great care must be taken not to cast a shadow over basking butterflies, not even over part of a wing, as this will usually send them dashing off. This can make it very difficult to obtain a good shot across the open wings of those species which orientate themselves carefully at right-angles to the sun when basking, for it is virtually impossible to approach without shading them at the last moment.

A tripod is more or less useless for butterfly photography in the field. It is heavy to carry around, while setting it up at the correct distance and height from your flighty subject is both clumsy and slow. We hand-hold all our insect shots, but for people with shaky hands a monopod can be useful; even a simple bamboo cane, which can be gripped in the left hand against the camera body to give a measure of support, will help. However, using a flash in dull conditions, such as those prevailing in a forest, should eliminate any difficulties with camera-shake, as the effective shutter speed will be the speed of the flash, usually between 1/800th and 1/1000th second for manual units, quite sufficient to freeze any vibrations from unsteady hands. The same applies to shooting with a zoom lens/flash combination in rather brighter conditions, but only if you are in possession of a camera such as the Nikon FM2 or FA which synchronise with flash at 1/250th second, although care should still be taken to hold the camera as still as possible. Close-ups at life-size or even larger, using a small flash or a ring-flash at f16 or so, should also pose no problems as the amount of available light striking the film will be overwhelmed by the light from the flash, thus avoiding a secondary daylight image. This can often lead to a surprising ability to freeze subject movement, permitting shots of male butterflies hovering in courtship over females.

Remember that in any kind of close-up work accurate focusing is of the utmost importance. Butterflies sitting with their wings outspread, or approached from the side if the wings are closed, are among the easier macro subjects. Their very flat presentation in these poses requires relatively little depth of field to achieve overall sharpness and an aperture of f11 is usually sufficient. Photographing butterflies head-on requires flash equipment capable of giving exposures of f16 or smaller, as you need a far greater depth of field to render both the head and the leading edges of the wings in sharp focus; achieving the latter is helped by concentrating on the eyes, or on the proboscis if the butterfly is feeding.

Many aspiring photographers forget that the background can add to or detract from the attractiveness of the finished picture to a surprising degree. Out-of-focus grass stems criss-crossing the area behind a butterfly feeding on a flower can prove to be very distracting, and pieces of vegetation protruding into the foreground even more so. A depth-of-field preview button on your camera comes into its own here, for blades of grass or twigs, unnoticed by you when focusing at full aperture, will be brought into sharp prominence as you briefly check the picture area by stopping down to the taking aperture.

Using electronic flash to photograph butterflies on flowers isolated at more than half a metre (½ yd) from surrounding vegetation will often result in a considerably darkened, even black, background. This upsets some people, who are often amazingly vociferous concerning the totally 'unnatural' nature of this type of background which has often been accused of making the pictures appear nocturnal. This is not entirely true, as photographing a butterfly by natural sunlight, as it sits feeding on a flower against a backcloth of dark, brooding woodland or even a bush, will give precisely the same results, since the difference in exposure between the well-lit butterfly and the poorly lit background can be four or five f stops. This results in the same dark background as sometimes occurs when flash is used. One of the best backgrounds against which to shoot butterflies is a blue sky but underexposing this looks terrible, as the shade of blue becomes totally unrealistic and looks completely wrong, especially as there is no natural way in which this can come about, in contradiction to the case cited above. When portraying a butterfly against blue sky it therefore pays to match the subject to the background by first taking a TTL reading of the sky's exposure. A clear blue, but not brilliant sky usually works out to an exposure of around 1/60th second at f11/16 with Kodachrome 64. A miniature flash unit, which gives precisely this exposure, can now be used to provide sparkling illumination for the butterfly. Readers with variable power flash units can simply switch to a lower power to give an acceptable match. In a similar way you can match flash-lit butterflies to a grassy, sunlit background, if this is your preference. However, when matching flash to available light, remember that under these circumstances your flash loses its ability to freeze movement, as a sunlit image of the butterfly will also appear on the final picture, along with the flash-lit image. This is called synchro-sunlight blur and it calls for extra care in avoiding camera and subject movement when shooting under bright conditions. For temperate butterflies engaged in nectaring on flowers, matching the two sources of light can often give the most rewarding results.

Appendices

A

Butterflies observed on a small piece of predator dung in Kakamega Forest, Kenya.

Charaxes pleione, C. brutus, C. etesipe, C. tiridates, Pseudacraea lucretia, Vanessula milca (all Nymphalidae).

B

Butterflies attracted to urine-soaked ground in Kakamega Forest, Kenya over a period of five days.

Nymphalidae: *Cymothoe lurida, C. hobarti, Pseudoathyma neptidina, Vanessula milca, Cyrestis camillus, Pseudacraea lucretia, Salamis parhassus, S. temora, Phalanta columbina, Hypolimnas dinarcha, Euphaedra zampa, Euriphene ribensis, Euryphura isuka, Junonia stygia, Euptera elabonitas, Acraea penelope, A. pharsalus.*
Papilionidae: *Papilio phorcas, P. jacksoni.*
Pieridae: *Belenois calypso minor.*
Also various **Lycaenidae**.

C

Butterflies on bare earth behind a hut in Tingo Maria, Peru. Only those which were actually photographed over a two-week period are listed. Many more species were present from time to time but resisted all attempts at photography.

Nymphalidae:
Nymphalinae: *Marpesia zerynthia dentigera, M. berania berania, M. crethon crethon, M. themistocles norica, Tritanessa teletusa, T. liriope* (in groups), *Hamadryas amethusa thearida, H. arinome anomala, Callicore hystaspes, Doxocopa cyane cyane, D. agathina agathina, D. elis fabaris, D. laurentia cherubina, Adelpha mesentina chancha, A. thessalia thessalia, Archonias bellona negrina, Smyrna blomfildia blomfildia, Memphis philomena philomena, Eresia etia etia.*
Heliconiinae: *Heliconius doris doris, H. wallacei flavescens.*
Ithomiinae: *Tithoria harmonia martina.*
Acraeinae: *Actinote alcione salmonea, A. negra sobrina.*
Riodininae: *Siseme neurodes caudalis, Rhetus periander laonome, Crocozona coecias coecias, Chalodeta theodora theodora, Dynamine mylitta, Caria mantinea.*

Pieridae: *Charonius theano eurytele, Hesperocharis nereina, Dismorphia lygdamis doris.*
Hesperiidae: *Oxynetra semihyalina, Pyrrhopyge sp., Jemadia sp., Phocides sp.,* (all brilliantly jewel-like).

Glossary

Alkaloid   Toxic substance produced by plants, e.g. strychnine.

Androconia   Special scales, found only in male butterflies, which disseminate **pheromones**.

Aposematic coloration   Bright colours which serve to warn predators of a possibly unpalatable butterfly.

Chitin   The main material forming the tough exoskeleton.

Cremaster   Hook on the tail end of the pupa by which it attaches itself to a silken pad adhering to a leaf, rock, etc.

Crypsis   Camouflage colouring which allows a butterfly or its immature stages to blend into its background.

Diapause   Any stage during a butterfly's life-cycle when development is temporarily suspended, usually during adverse climatic conditions.

Dimorphism   Usually sexual dimorphism, the existence of marked differences between the sexes in colour, pattern or structure.

Eclosion   Emergence of the tiny caterpillar from the egg or the adult butterfly from the pupa.

Flicker-vision   Someone with good flicker-vision would be able to pick out the individual frames while watching a cine film, instead of seeing them all running into each other.

Frass   Waste products from the butterfly caterpillar.

Hair-pencils   Tufts of hairs on the end of the abdomen of some male butterflies. These may be extruded from a small sac and are used to help in the dissemination of **androconia**.

Instar   Any one of the stages between moults in the growth of the butterfly larva.

Love-dust   *See* **androconia**.

Neotropical   Describes the zoogeographic region encompassing all of South and much of Central America.

Parasitoid   Larva of wasp or fly which lives inside one of the stages of the butterfly life-cycle, most commonly the caterpillar. It feeds on its host's tissues, eventually causing its death.

Pheromone   A volatile, air-borne chemical messenger, often used to attract members of the opposite sex.

Sequester   The obtaining from plants of chemicals which the butterfly then uses to defend itself against the unwelcome attentions of its enemies.

Spermatophore   A packet of sperm passed on to the female by the male during copulation.

Guide to Further Reading

There are many books on butterflies but the following are a good starting point for delving more deeply into their biology.

D'Abrera, B. (2001), *Concise Atlas of Butterflies of the World*, Hill House Publishers, Melbourne.
Lewis, H.L. (2000), *Butterflies of the World*, Broken Books, London.
Owen, D.F. (1971), *Tropical Butterflies: The Ecology and Behaviour of Butterflies in the Tropics with Special Reference to African Species*, Oxford University Press, London
Sbordoni, V. and Forestiero, S. (1998), *Butterflies of the World*, Firefly Books.
Scott, J.A. (1992), *The Butterflies of North America*, Stanford University Press, Palo Alto, California.
Vane-Wright, R.I. and Ackery, P.R. (ed.) (1984), *The Biology of Butterflies*, Symposium of the Royal Entomological Society of London, Number 11, Academic Press Inc. (London) Ltd., London.

Butterfly Conservation Societies

Readers are urged to join one of the following societies dedicated to the conservation of butterflies.

British Butterfly Conservation Society, Tudor House, Quorn, nr. Loughborough, Leics, LE12 8AD, UK
The Xerces Society, 10 Southwest Ash Street, Portland, Oregon 97024

Picture Credits

All photographs courtesy of Premaphotos Wildlife.

Index

Numbers in *italics* refer to black and white illustrations.
Numbers in **bold** refer to colour plates.